PRISON PAPERS

PAPERS

FROM A CAPTIVE AMBASSADOR

PRISON
PAPERS
FROM A CAPTIVE AMBASSADOR

MARIO VELOSO

Pacific Press Publishing Association
Boise, Idaho
Montemorelos, Nuevo Leon, Mexico
Oshawa, Ontario, Canada

4418

Designed by Tim Larson
Cover Photos by Duane Tank

Copyright © 1985 by
Pacific Press Publishing Association
Printed in United States of America

Library of Congress Cataloging in Publication Data

Veloso, Mario.
  Prison papers.

  1. Bible. N. T. Ephesians—Criticism, interpretation, etc. I. Title.
BX2695.2.V45   1985   227'.506   85-534
ISBN 0-8163-0601-X

85 86 87 88 89 • 6 5 4 3 2 1

Contents

How to Know the Will of God

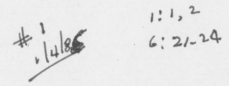

Human beings are making their way through a dark tunnel, so to speak. Many are groping their way with a flickering lantern of personal ideas. Others grope along in the lightning flash of scientific knowledge. The lanterns do not shed sufficient light to make things clear, and the bright flashes of lightning give only momentary insights. Neither of these sources of illumination are of any real help. Unaided by the light of God's Word, even professed Christians walk in darkness. They cannot discern the true significance of life. They cannot understand the will of God. However, there is no need for the Christian to live in uncertainty, because God has "made known unto us the mystery of his will" (Ephesians 1:9) in the Bible.

To "the princes of this world" the wisdom of God is a mystery (1 Corinthians 2:7, 8), but it has been revealed to those who accept the gospel "and the preaching of Jesus Christ" (Romans 16:25). Only the initiated Christian knows God's will. To this class of Christians, Paul writes what William Barclay calls "the queen of the epistles"—*The Epistle to the Ephesians*.

This letter is divided into two parts. Chapters 1 to 3 deal with doctrine; chapters 4 to 6 speak about conduct. Paul begins the epistle with a greeting (Ephesians 1:1, 2), then writes an extensive doxology, a praise to God in which he explains what the will of God the Father is toward us in Christ, the Beloved (Verses 3-14).

God Shows His Will by What He Does for Us

Throughout the Bible God is revealed as a God of action. He is depicted as the omnipotent Creator and Sustainer of His creation.

At the same time the Word of God describes Him as a compassionate God, one who is always close to His creatures; a wise God who reveals truth; a loving God who is interested in each of us individually, who helps us and saves us; a merciful God, full of goodness, the One who loves the sinner.

The God revealed in the Bible never fails. He is not an arbitrary Lord, an Almighty Potentate lacking benevolence. He is not an I AM in absentia, a corrupted Saint, a covetous El-shaddai. He is a God who always satisfies. As El-shaddai, the God of inexhaustible riches, the Omnipotent, the God of all power and authority, He reveals His will through His acts of beneficence, election, and predestination. Paul assures the Ephesians of this fact in verses 3-6.

Through His blessings, God wants us to be spiritually-minded. Paul declares, "Blessed be the God and Father of our Lord Jesus Christ, who hath blessed us with all spiritual blessings in heavenly places in Christ." Verse 3. God has revealed the fact that He wants to impart His spiritual blessing to us. His are not carnal blessings.

There are no carnal blessings promised the carnal man for the simple reason that God's blessings are both a spiritual gift and a relationship. As *gifts* they are abundant. They include, for instance, the use and control of the powers of procreation in harmony with His divine purpose, the power to exercise mastery over the earth without destroying it, and the capacity to exercise compassionate dominion over every living creature. See Genesis 1:28-30.

As a *relationship* God's blessings are spiritual. When God blesses, the recipient and the Donor are brought into a close relationship. They are knit firmly together by the spiritual element present in the blessing. As God gives the blessing and the individual accepts it, a two-way communication is produced which creates true spiritual communion and understanding.

The person comes to realize what God wants him to be, a Christian in spirit, and it is his desire to be just that. He knows that God has done for him that which he "could not do" without divine help—keep the divine law. See Romans 8:1-3. Now everything that was impossible in his spiritual life becomes possible.

The difficulty impossible to resolve, the temptation impossible to resist, the weakness impossible to overcome, the attitude impossible to change, the identification with God and His church impossible to achieve, <u>all this and much more besides becomes possible in Christ Jesus</u>.

The spiritual blessing permits us to do that which is impossible by any other means. It results in a remarkable transformation that takes place in our thoughts, our actions, and our attitudes. See Romans 8:5-10. God's will for us is to enable us to do that which is naturally impossible.

Through His blessings God says to us, "I want you to live after the Spirit. Don't be rebellious when things don't go just the way you would like them to go. I want you to learn how to understand My will because the man of God discerns the things of the Spirit."

Through His election, His choice, God wants us to be holy. The apostle Paul continues his letter to the Ephesians by saying, "He hath chosen us in him before the foundation of the world, that we should be holy and without blame before him in love." Ephesians 1:4. Through His election, God expresses His original will and plan for us human beings. God chose us as individuals to be holy, without one stain of sin. He chose us as a community to make up His people. In Old Testament times His community was called Israel; today it is known as the church.

The main point of emphasis in this election is that it is a relationship originating with God and that it has a specific objective. God initiates this election. He is the one who elects, who chooses. But it is not an arbitrary or capricious choice on God's part, by which some are elected to eternal life and others are condemned to perdition.

So far as individuals are concerned, the objective of the election is their sanctification, a life without the blemishes of sin. In the case of the community—ancient Israel and the Christian church—God chose them as a group to serve Him. God elected a particular community, a "chosen generation" to "shew forth the praises of him" who called them "out of darkness into his marvellous light." 1 Peter 2:9.

Through election, God expresses His will for each individual as well as for His church. He wants every Christian to be holy, and He wants His church to be faithful in fulfilling the mission He has entrusted to it.

Through predestination God wants us to be His children. Through election God expresses His will so that the Christian leads a holy life and the church is an active missionary-minded community.

Predestination expresses God's will regarding the Christian. He wants him to be His child. "Having predestinated us unto the adoption of children by Jesus Christ to himself, according to the good pleasure of his will, to the praise of the glory of his grace, wherein he hath made us accepted in the beloved." Ephesians 1:5, 6.

Throughout the centuries theologians have tried to solve the problem of predestination, but generally speaking, they have not been very successful. The reason is that usually they have approached the problem from the wrong angle. They assume that a prior predestination is the divine method by which individuals are saved or lost. The Bible, however, does not teach predestination as a *method*. It uses the word to refer to God's *objective* in His redemptive acts. Paul identifies these redemptive acts of God in his letter to the Romans.

The sequence of God's redeeming actions is here clearly defined. First, He knows the individual. Building upon this knowledge, His second act is to predestinate him. Third, He calls the individual. Fourth, He justifies him. And finally, He glorifies him. See Romans 8:28-30. Predestination is not an arbitrary act on God's part. To be predestined does not mean that a person is born with his destiny already marked out for him. By the same token, a person is not born justified, nor does he come into the world glorified.

Predestination, according to the Bible, is the expression of God's will for all human beings. Paul declares in 1 Timothy 2:4 that God "will have all men to be saved." This is God's expressed will. Second Peter 3:9 puts it this way: "The Lord . . . is longsuffering to us-ward, not willing that any should perish, but that all should come to repentance." (Compare with Titus 2:11.) God wants to claim every one of us as His children. But we can become sons and daughters of God only as we accept His universal offer of salvation through faith, "For ye are all the children of God by faith in Christ Jesus." Galatians 3:26. God expresses His will for us through predestination, but He does not arbitrarily dictate what our choice will be.

Through His blessings God says to us, "I want you to walk in the Spirit." Through election He declares, "I want you to be holy, and I want my church to have missionary spirit." By predestinating us He affirms, "I want you to be my child." In declarations God expresses three things that He wants to do for us: He wants to give, so He gives us His abundant spiritual blessings; He wants to transform, so He transforms us from lost sinners into saints without a single blemish of sin; He wants to adopt, so He adopts us as His sons and daughters in Christ Jesus.

God Shows His Will in What Christ Does for Us

The Bible declares that Christ has done many things for us. In all these things He fulfilled the will of His Father; therefore, what Christ has done for us is, at the same time, what the Father has done on our behalf. The apostle Paul sums up this truth in two points—redemption and inheritance. See Ephesians 1:7-12.

Through redemption God expressed His desire that we be free to live a meaningful life. The apostle Peter declares, "You were redeemed from the empty way of life." 1 Peter 1:18, NIV. We were ransomed from a life-style that offers nothing, that produces nothing. It was empty. But Christ saved us. He became the gift of God for us. He freed us from the meaningless life.

God, in redeeming us in Christ Jesus, expresses His will that we be free, that we live a life full of meaning. When He gives us this life, He also gives us the knowledge of "the mystery of his will, according to his good pleasure which he hath purposed in himself: that in the dispensation of the fulness of times he might gather together in one all things in Christ, both which are in heaven, and which are on earth." Ephesians 1:9, 10. God wants us to live in unity. Cosmic unity, in heaven and on earth. Communal unity in the church. Familial unity in the Christian family. Spiritual unity in the heart of each believer. Unity with God in each one of His children.

Skilled musicians are able to create delightful harmonies. Those who are not musically talented marvel at the beautiful strains musicians produce and wonder how they accomplish this. But far more marvelous and mysterious is the harmony God can create in our lives. When He redeems us, He not only pardons our transgressions, but grants the power to overcome sin. He breaks the power of our vain frivolities, our mental anguish, our confusion, our emotional disturbances, our mixed-up ways of doing what we should not and not doing what we should.

God redeems us, He gives us liberty, He saves us in order to be able to unite us with Himself and His cosmic family. He wants all of us to be one in Christ Jesus.

God also expresses His will by giving us an inheritance. See verses 11, 12. The Greeks had two words for *inheritance*. Both terms were derived from the same root, *kleros*. One refers to an inheritance received, the other, to the act of becoming part of a group. In English "inheritance" is what a rich relative leaves to his survivors—money, property, heirlooms. We have all heard people say, "I don't have a rich uncle to leave me anything!"

It gives one a warm feeling to be part of a group and to feel totally accepted by all its members. I belong to such a marvelous group. I am part of the Seventh-day Adventist Church. I would not exchange this feeling of belonging for anything else in the whole world. Admittedly we sometimes go through difficult experiences. What group doesn't? It is true that all of us have not experienced all the spiritual blessings that are ours. Sometimes there are misunderstandings. Sometimes there are jealousies. Sometimes there are animosities and grudges. These problems should not exist among us, yet they do, and we should perseveringly strive to work them out. God wants us to be included in His inheritance, to be part of His people, to be members of His group, to have a part in His church. A member of the remnant church should never feel alone, distressed, or rejected. By the same token, he must never cause a fellow church member to feel alone, distressed, or rejected.

The members of Christ's body should live in unity. We must feel that we are part of the group. We must be totally integrated in the church. We are the inheritance of the Lord. The church is our very own inheritance.

When God says that He wants us as <u>His heirs</u>, He is expressing His desire to eliminate every painful situation in our relationships with others. He wants us to live in complete unity with one another. Why does God want us as His heirs? To show His glory. "That we should be to the praise of his glory, who first trusted in Christ." Verse 12. See also John 17:21, 22.

God Shows His Will in What the Holy Spirit Does for Us

According to the Epistle to the Ephesians, the glory of God is the manifestation of His attributes. When His attributes are recognized by us, and clearly evident in us, the glory of God is made manifest to those about us.

How is this accomplished? By the sealing of the Spirit. A sealing that is brought about by being attentive to the Word and by believing in Christ Jesus. When we listen carefully with an obedient ear, with an ear that accepts what it hears, with an ear that incorporates the Word of God into the life, when we, through this life-giving hearing, arrive at the communion of faith, at an intimate relationship of faith with Christ, then we are sealed by the Holy Spirit. That seal is the mark that makes it official, that gives it authenticity.

The seal of the Holy Spirit is not like that which the government or some other entity uses; neither is it like the seal used by an educational institution, without which the academic certificates would have no value whatever. The seal of the Holy Spirit is a living seal. It consists of imparting God's attributes to our lives. It places those attributes in us and causes them to be reflected in our lives. When these attributes are present in our lives a transformation becomes apparent.

We live to the glory of God because His attributes are manifest and we reveal His will to others. Our lives make these attributes visible and comprehensible. Without the Spirit such attributes would never become a part of our character. How could we be good without the Spirit dwelling in us? How could we be loving and kind to others without the presence of the Spirit? Without the Spirit, religion would be a formal hypocrisy.

With the seal of the Spirit, God grants us a foretaste of redemption—an anticipation of that life we will have in the future. Even though immortality is conferred upon the righteous at the second coming, eternal life begins here and now. It must become a reality in each Christian. The sealing work expresses the will of God by the manifestation of His glory through us and by the inheritance that awaits us.

The Spirit is the guarantee of the inheritance. See verses 13, 14. We have the assurance that eternal life will be ours and that it begins right now. We have the surety of salvation. It is not the surety that gives one the false confidence that once he is saved he is always saved. It is the surety of faith. We are related to Christ by faith, and the Spirit guarantees the reality of this relationship. We receive the promise of life eternal, and the Spirit guarantees that this will be ours. In this sense, because we are related to Christ and because He never fails, we have the surety of salvation. The Spirit offers that surety to our minds.

The Holy Spirit carries out the sealing work and represents the guarantee of the inheritance. Through these works of the Holy Spirit, God expresses His will for us. God wants us to be part of the group that makes up His inheritance, in other words, His church. He also desires His attributes to be incorporated into our lives, and He wants us to have the surety of salvation by faith.

God's will, as expressed in the doxology of the Epistle to the Ephesians, is for us to be spiritually-minded, to be holy, to be His sons and daughters, to be free to participate in all His works, to belong to His group, the church, to have His attributes in our lives, and to have the surety of salvation.

How do we carry out the will of God? There is a phrase in Paul's doxology that describes how this happens. It is "in Christ." All the spiritual blessings are in Christ. God chose us in Him. He predestined us in the Beloved. In Him we have redemption. In Him we are made heirs and are sealed in Christ. All is possible when we are in Him.

What does it mean to be in Christ? Spiritually, it means to be in harmony with Him and His will. Visibly, it means to belong to His church. "To him be glory *in the church* and *in Christ Jesus* to all generations, for ever and ever. Amen." Ephesians 3:21, RSV, emphasis supplied. To be in Christ and to be in the church is one and the same thing because the church is the body of Christ and Christ is the head of the church.

What Is the Knowledge of God?

(handwritten: # 2 1/11/86   1:3 - 14)

In this chapter we will study one of Paul's prayers. Recorded in Ephesians 1, it is the prayer of a church leader on behalf of the members of the church, whom he dearly loves. If someone were to ask the apostle Paul what two things he loved most, he would answer, "Christ and His church." Every true Seventh-day Adventist Christian who is asked the same question should be able to give the same reply. Such a person identifies with Christ; he identifies with His church. To him Christ and His church are inseparable. There is a special kind of knowledge involved in this relationship. Paul begins his prayer by speaking of "knowledge" and concludes it by referring to the church, the "body" of Christ and "the fulness of him that filleth all in all." Ephesians 1:23.

Paul's prayer is expressed in a single sentence, which begins with verse 15 and continues to verse 23. His prayer proceeds from speaking of God to speaking of God's church. This suggests that one who joins the church cannot remain in ignorance of God. In other words, a Christian cannot be a faithful church member and at the same time be ignorant of those things that pertain to God.

Intercessory Prayer

Intercessory prayer is essential to the Christian life. Such prayer creates spiritual unity among the believers, while at the same time it creates unity between the believers and God. This is the kind of prayer Paul prayed on behalf of the Ephesians. He

17

begins by saying, "Wherefore," in other words, "For this reason" (RSV).

For what reason? In order to answer this question we must examine the context that precedes the statement. The apostle says that he prays for the Ephesian brethren because they know the will of God and have the experience of unity in Christ Jesus; they have redemption, an inheritance, and the seal; they have faith in the Lord Jesus and love toward all the saints. For these reasons, then, Paul says, I "cease not to give thanks for you, making mention of you in my prayers." Verse 16.

Intercessory prayer is usually made because a problem exists. But it should not be just a request for a solution to the problem. It should also be an expression of gratitude. Paul's prayer expresses this latter element. He thanks God for the Ephesians. He is grateful that they do not have spiritual problems. They have faith in the Lord and show their love to all the saints. This twofold relationship—faith in God and love for the church members—comprises the foundation upon which the knowledge of God is built.

Two basic themes are in Paul's continual intercessory prayers for the Ephesians—knowledge of God and the power He has given to His church.

Knowledge With an Objective

Paul does not pray that the believers might know what the knowledge of God *consists of*. This would be objective knowledge—knowledge observed at a distance. Such knowledge is like knowing what bread consists of by reading about it in a book. Paul wants his readers to know by actual experience. To accomplish this objective, Paul tells us *why* we should have an experiential knowledge of God and *how* we may obtain it.

First: how do we acquire such knowledge? The apostle tells us—through wisdom, revelation, and enlightenment. See verses 17, 18.

Wisdom, as used by Paul, is spiritual comprehension as evidenced in the behavior. Revelation is a direct communication from God to human beings. Illumination enlightens the thoughts and the whole personality. God is the One who brings all this about. He is the originator of knowledge; He transmits it; He places it in the mind; and He is the One who transforms the behavior. It is a dynamic knowledge.

Wisdom, revelation, and illumination produce two kinds of learning. The first is called "knowledge." Verse 17. The second is referred to as comprehension or "understanding." Verse 18. The word translated "knowledge" refers to that kind of knowledge that has a purpose or objective. It is not merely the acquisition of information nor an accumulation of facts. It is completely different from that kind of knowledge which is simply an accumulation of information and data about God. The kind of knowledge Paul is talking about is acquired by means of wisdom, and wisdom has to do with a person's conduct. So, Paul is writing about knowledge that affects our conduct. It means that we know God in such a way that He controls our actions. This is the kind of knowledge that enables us to live a good life. God modifies our conduct, controls it, and harmonizes it with His will.

When the sinner receives Christ, he obtains salvation and with salvation he receives abundant wisdom. Verses 7-9. Wisdom comes from God (verse 17) and is communicated through His church (Ephesians 3:10). Wisdom gives us a knowledge of that which is "good." Romans 16:19. Evil does not control the lives of those who are wise. We understand good and evil here in the highest and yet simplest sense of these words. The knowledge of God through wisdom helps the person in his daily life, in the common activities of his existence. It gives the child of God peace, security, and confidence in what he is doing. Such knowledge comes as a result of the salvation he has obtained in Christ Jesus. Ephesians 1: 7, 8.

Knowledge with an objective in mind is different from an accumulated store of information, not only because it includes wisdom in its makeup, but also because it comes through a process of revelation. In the writings of Paul we see that revelation is the means by which God communicates His mysteries to the true Christian. Through revelation the Christian receives knowledge that other human beings do not have. Through revelation, the Christian perceives the call of God, the gospel, the judgment of God, and especially, "the mystery hidden for ages and generations." Colossians 1:26, RSV. See also Galatians 1:12; Romans 2:5; 16:25; Ephesians 3:3.

In the Epistle to the Ephesians there are several references to this mystery. Paul refers to it when he states that the Jews and the Gentiles, who were formerly separated, should become a single people, united in the church through the preaching of the gospel. The knowledge of the mystery of God is the revelation of the gospel which serves to hold the church together as a unit. The revelation of God is a form of knowledge that has as its goal the unification of His people. Actually it is a knowledge having two objectives: saving and uniting.

Christ, in His prayer in John 17, referred to this unity as the most effective instrument for the preaching of the gospel. If the church does not experience complete unity—in doctrine, structure, conduct, leadership, in having a strong missionary spirit—it needs more fully to acquire the knowledge of God through revelation. Allowed its proper function, this knowledge purges everything that comes from human sources. Revelation has only one true source—God. Attempts to mix divine knowledge with worldly knowledge corrupts the former so that it is no longer divine knowledge. The resultant knowledge destroys unity, and, as a result, the missionary power and strength of the church is diminished.

According to Paul, true knowledge does not divide the church; rather it creates unity. It makes the work of the church more effective. The true knowledge of God causes the church to become a more living, vibrant body, enjoying the full presence of Christ. Thus, the church has such spiritual vitality and power and is so marvelously alive, that it is active in bearing the good news of the gospel to every soul who is in need of it.

The second kind of knowledge that Paul prays for on behalf of the church is "understanding", or comprehension *(eidénai)* Ephesians 1:18. This is the living knowledge that enables one initiated in the "mystery" of the gospel to discern the true significance of something—its clearly defined meaning. Understanding has two basic elements: It is a living force and it is meaningful. The intellect does not perceive this knowledge; it is realized in the life. This is the knowledge acquired from a person as we live with that individual. It is not the knowledge that is told to us or that we can obtain through reading; it is the knowledge of God obtained by living with Him.

When God becomes Someone very dear to us, Someone we love, Someone with whom we want to live every moment of our lives and whom we come to know by experiencing His actions for and through us, He will not be a far-away, distant God. He will be a very present God—real, living, vibrant. We will walk with Him and we will live for Him.

With this kind of knowledge, each member of the church, and the Adventist community as a whole, will constantly radiate a winsome influence on those about them. Such knowledge engenders in the recipient a desire to communicate that which it has received—a meaningful revelation of the gospel. This imparted knowledge, in turn, will exert a magnetic attraction on still others.

The gospel reaches the depths of the heart and penetrates the bones down to the marrow because it transforms one completely. This knowledge is obtained by *illumination*. Paul is not referring here to the intellect or the mind. If so, he would be dealing with a rationalistic knowledge. Christians may have a rational knowledge of God and His truth, but this is too limited a knowledge. Paul asks for an illumination that embraces much more than the mind. He asks for illumination of the heart. This includes the illumination of the intellect, the emotions, and the will. He wants a knowledge of God that is a total experience. A true knowledge of God can never be partial. It is a complete knowledge and comes with a complete life.

That is why God is deeply concerned when He sees a man who is divided in his allegiance. God was not pleased when Israel was partially dedicated to the pagan gods and partially dedicated to Him. God accepts only total dedication.

Now we must ask ourselves, For what purpose do we obtain the knowledge of God? What is the goal God has in mind when He communicates this life-giving knowledge with an objective?

The first objective of knowledge is the "calling." This is a knowledge that produces a calling. It does not have to do with a calling that seeks for knowledge in order to carry it out. We do not obtain knowledge by having a calling. We go to God and He gives us the calling. This is communication, a commitment, a relationship of hearing and obeying and being in company with God. The calling is from God and the response from man. Of all the elements that comprise the calling, Paul picks out one in particular—hope. He says in his prayer, "that ye may know what is the hope of his calling." Ephesians 1:18.

All true hope has something for the present as well as something for the future. Hope that does not have something for the present is meaningless. And hope that has nothing for the future is empty. Christian hope has a surety for the present and real substance for the future.

Christian hope for the present is so wonderful that Paul calls it the "hope of glory" and identifies it with Christ living in us. God wants His saints to "make known what is the riches of the glory of this mystery among the Gentiles; which is Christ in you, the hope of glory." Colossians 1:27. This hope of glory is Christ in us. We must not forget that the ultimate objective of the knowledge of God, according to Paul's teaching in this part of his epistle, is the church. Only when Christ is really in us, can we really be in His church. This true spiritual unity with Christ and His church constitutes the present surety of hope.

The reality of the Christian's future hope is so abundant that Paul calls it "that blessed hope." He identifies it with the second coming of Christ. He says, "Looking for that blessed hope, and the glorious appearing of the great God and our Saviour Jesus Christ; who gave himself for us, that he might redeem us from all iniquity, and purify unto himself a peculiar people, zealous of good works." Titus 2:13, 14.

The second objective of the knowledge of God is the inheritance. He gives us the knowledge of Him so that we may know "the riches of the glory of his inheritance in the saints." Ephesians 1:18. Paul had already spoken to the Ephesians about inheritance when he referred to belonging to the Christian group. Now he uses the other word. Inheritance as a possession. It is the same inheritance mentioned by Peter when he says, "We have been born anew . . . to an inheritance . . . kept in heaven for you." 1 Peter 1:3, 4, RSV. Paul does not forget the heritage which is ours now. He alludes to this fact in the phrase "in the saints." We have an inheritance "in the saints" and an inheritance in heaven—one of belonging, the other of possessing. The inheritance has this double measure. We belong to a group that possesses something. The knowledge of God makes us be part of the group and gives us the right to possess all that God bestows in heaven and the new earth.

When Paul speaks of the inheritance in its twofold dimension, he is referring to one specific element in it. To "the riches of the glory" of the inheritance. The expression "riches" is linked to the inheritance. It is speaking of receiving the future kingdom. The expression "glory" is linked to "the saints." Throughout the entire Epistle to the Ephesians, and in many other texts in the New Testament, we find that the glory of God is His character. The characteristics of an heir to the inheritance from God—the church—and who receives the possessions of His inheritance—the kingdom of heaven—shows this by character developed in him. The glory of the inheritance is the character of the Christian—the character of God reflected in us by the action of the Holy Spirit. The church demonstrates to the world the character of God. The best way to glorify God is not through words spoken to His glory but by a character that reflects the attributes of the character of God.

The Christian inheritance is the church as well as the kingdom of God. Being in the church anticipates being in the kingdom. Whoever wants to have a part in God's future kingdom must belong to His church now. None of this would be possible without the action of the power of God.

The third objective of the knowledge of God is the manifestation of His power. Paul prays that the saints may know "the exceeding greatness of his power to us-ward who believe, according to the working of his mighty power." Ephesians 1:19.

The power of God, specifically "the exceeding greatness of his power," brought into effect three things: Christ's resurrection, His enthronement, and His supremacy. He was resurrected from the dead, He was seated at the right hand of God, and all things in heaven and in earth have been put under His feet. See also 1 Corinthians 15:27, 28.

The fact that the power of God was manifest in resurrecting Christ indicates that, likewise, when we die and are placed in the grave, one day we will be resurrected so that we may be forever with the Lord. See 1 Thessalonians 4:14.

The power of God gave Christ the supremacy "far above all principality, and power, and might, and dominion, and every name that is named, not only in this world, but also in that which is to come." Ephesians 1:21. This is the power of rulership. He conceded the authority to Him to whom it belonged, and put each being in the place that truly belonged to him, in the plan He had for the universe. No created being will ever again make the pretentious claims that Satan made. Everyone will be satisfied with his own sphere. No being will ever again rebel against the power and authority of Christ as ruler of the universe.

The Supreme Power in the Church

Paul's presentation concerning the knowledge of God with an objective is now coming to its conclusion. That knowledge, which, as has been pointed out, is obtained by wisdom, by revelation, and by illumination; that knowledge which manifests itself in behavior, in the mind, in the sentiments, in the will, in the whole personality; that knowledge which is granted as hope in the calling, riches in the inheritance, and the fullness of power, has as its objective, the church. God delivers all power to Christ, and He as Lord over death, as Intercessor for sinners, and as Ruler of the universe, is made "the head over all things for the church, which is his body, the fullness of him who fills all in all." Ephesians 1:22, 23 RSV.

The church is the only place on earth where the fullness of the power of God is manifest. All mankind can enjoy that same power. They need only the knowledge of God that leads them to Christ. By that same power they will become part of Christ. Not in a mystical and esoteric manner, but in a simple, yet certain, way. Human beings are part of Christ when they become an integral part of His body, the church. The same power that actuates Christ actuates them also. That power which belongs to Christ belongs to them as well, because they are part of the body of which Christ is the head. Therefore, those who are in Christ, who are an integral part of the church community possess the same omnipotent power of God that Christ possesses.

The knowledge of God is not simple information. The knowledge of God is experiencing the hope of His calling and responding to that call with hope, with action, with dedication of the life and receiving the inheritance.

The action of the supreme power of God on behalf of mankind brings them to Christ. It incorporates them into the church in order that they may form part of the body of Christ. This power transforms them into coheirs with Christ, members of His family and true possessors of all the things that are in God and that God possesses in the entire universe.

A mystery? Perhaps so. But at the same time it is a very concrete reality when it comes to all the benefits we enjoy as part of Christ's body. Religion, then, is not a piece of information for the mind. It is a way of life which includes all that we are, all that we do, all our hopes and aspirations, all the moments of our lives. The knowledge of God, which leads us into this experience with Christ, is a valid reality for today and for the future. In the present it leads us to an encounter with Christ in His Church. In the future it leads us to an encounter with Christ throughout eternity in His kingdom.

What It Means to Be With Christ

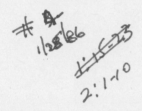

We know that every Christian has to be with Christ, but what does this mean? We hear this phrase often, but it can still be meaningless to us. It is unfortunate that some things lose their meaning by constant repetition. When this happens, one's religion becomes dull and lifeless. It becomes merely a habit, a custom. It has lost its luster and true significance.

We shall now consider the third part of the Epistle to the Ephesians (2:1-10). It speaks about being "with Christ." Why does the apostle address this subject? In the second part of the epistle, he explained the knowledge of God and how this knowledge leads us to the church. This knowledge is wisdom, revelation, and illumination. It includes the behavior and the thoughts. The entire personality. The whole being. This knowledge leads us to the experience of the calling of God and, specifically, to the hope of the calling. It leads us to the inheritance with the saints and, particularly, to the glory of that inheritance which is our conduct among the saints and will take us to the eternal kingdom. Finally, it will permit us to receive the power of God. The power wrought in Christ, which resurrected Him from the dead, enthroned Him in heaven, and "appointed him as supreme head to the church." Ephesians 1:22, NEB.

After his exposition on the knowledge of God, Paul turns his attention to the believers, pointing out to them that "you hath he quickened" (Ephesians 2:1) even as God raised Christ to life again. He resurrected Christ, and He raises us—"raised us up with him." Ephesians 2:6, RSV. Let us notice the connection: life-power was wrought in Christ, resurrecting Him; and life-power is wrought in us for our own resurrection.

Spiritual Death and Physical Death

Then Paul explains why God gives us life, saying, because "we were dead in sins." Ephesians 2:5. We were dead in our trespasses and sins. It is evident he is not talking about the death of the grave. Here he is speaking of living people who are dead. All of us are familiar with the spiritual death one goes through from a guilty conscience or when one suffers from the negative aspects of life, such as anxiety, worry, frustration, uncertainty— all the disease-causing things people subject themselves to that finally result in death. People in this condition cannot enjoy life. It is possible they never truly experienced real living. Ephesians 2:1.

"Dead in trespasses and sins." Paul told the Colossians, "You are dead in your sins and in the uncircumcision." Colossians 2:13, NIV. When he speaks of sins, he is referring to the sins of the Gentiles. Uncircumcision was a sin of which only an Israelite could be guilty. But spiritually all human beings are dead. Dead on account of the sins and trespasses in which they *"walked"* in times past. Ephesians 2:2. Not walked, or lived, sporadically, but continually. Walking suggests continuous action. That was the experience in the past. That walking in sin was "following the course of this world, following the prince of the power of the air, the spirit that is now at work in the sons of disobedience." Ephesians 2:2, RSV. To be dead in trespasses and sins and to be the children of disobedience is one and the same thing.

Children of Disobedience

What does the expression "children of disobedience" mean? It means to be "the children of wrath." Ephesians 2:3. Deserving the wrath of God. And why do they deserve God's wrath? Because of their worldliness and their indulgence in the desires of the flesh. Worldliness brings about disobedience and the desires of the flesh, in other words, the sexual sins.

Disobedience adversely affects our personality. All of us can remember the times when we were disobedient as children. When we had done something wrong we shrank from facing our parents. We felt uncomfortable. We did not want to be in their presence; we wanted to run away, to hide. We felt and acted different from the way we normally did. As adults we do the same thing when we disobey.

Disobedience produces something negative in the life, in the person, in the personality, in the emotions, in the sentiments, in the personal feeling of security. The entire personality seems to disintegrate when a person becomes a child of wrath. Sometimes such people do not recognize the condition they are in, yet they feel the effects that result from disobedience even in this life. This is not ordinary punishment, but punishment that is the result of divine wrath. Such a person is as though he were already dead. Even though he is alive he is not enjoying life in its true sense.

The "desires of the flesh" (Ephesians 2:3) affects the thoughts, the will, and the actions. When Paul uses this expression he is referring to sexual sins. The word in the original text should be translated "lust." This sin is more than the sin of desire; it inclines the will toward this type of illicit activity. The thoughts and the mental capacity are all under the control of sexual impulses. This uncontrollable desire makes one do things that separate him from God—he becomes distant from God. People who commit these sins deserve the wrath of God and become the "children of wrath."

God Gave Us Life

God, being rich in mercy, through His great love with which He loved us, while we were in this situation, "made us alive together with Christ." Ephesians 2:5, RSV. The Greek text holds more meaning than this translation suggests. Christ does three things for us: He gives us life, resurrects us from death, and lets us be with Him on His throne. See Ephesians 2:5, 6. From the experience of being a lost soul, we are elevated to a place where we recover life—life in all its dimensions, life as a Christian experience, as a satisfying existence, with prolongation of days into eternity; life in its fullness; life that comes from Christ.

Our spiritual resurrection is accomplished by the same power that raised Christ from the dead. If resurrection means consciousness to those who are raised from physical death, spiritual resurrection means a new consciousness to those who are raised to spiritual life through the new birth. Such a person can now think thoughts that before were foolishness to him. See 1 Corinthians 2:14. This resurrection is not only a promise of the future resurrection after we have been laid to rest, it is a present act of God's power taking place in us so that our spiritual life surges up in all its vitality.

We also receive authority. This is not authority over people. It is better than that. It is authority over the spiritual powers that have a negative influence over us. It is the authority over the devil, over his angels, and over all their temptations. Now they cannot overcome us. Now we are not alone. We are with Christ.

Together With Christ

In order to obtain life, resurrection, and authority, we need to be with Christ. We receive these things together with Him. Paul adds, We are made to "sit with him in the heavenly places in Christ Jesus." Ephesians 2:6, RSV. The demoniacal powers can conquer us only when we are not with Christ. Anyone who attempts to battle these forces in his own strength is doomed to failure.

I have listened to hundreds of young people describe their conflicts with evil habits. I have heard them tell about their victories and their defeats. Some have discovered the secret to a victorious Christian life, but many have not. But in my experience, the saddest thing is to see someone trying to fight his battles alone. Many fight alone, thinking all the time that Christ is with them in the struggle, when He is not. When temptation comes, these poor souls at first resist, but eventually succumb to Satan's cunning devices. At the close of the day, when they retire, they kneel down and tell God what happened. They tell him that they were defeated and ask Him to forgive them. This happens again and again. What is the problem? They fight alone. They think they are with Christ, but in this they are deceived. After praying to Him, they leave Him. They go to Him in defeat, but they are not with Him in the fight.

To be with Christ means to be with Him at all times—even when we are in the midst of temptation. How can we have this experience? We may have it very simply. Talk to Christ at the very time temptation strikes and ask Him to help you right then. Don't wait until afterwards to pray. Talk to Him immediately. Tell Him about your inner feelings that draw you toward temptation. Tell Him all that is happening and pray for strength—and strength will come! As we do this, we will always be with Him and we cannot be defeated.

How tragic it is when Christians try to conquer evil all by themselves. They are forever weakening and giving in. But this does not have to happen. If we maintained an unbroken relationship with Christ, we would always be victorious; for He is able to keep us from falling. See Jude 24. When we fall, it is never Christ's fault; it is ours. He possesses infinite power to help us, but we fail to avail ourselves of it.

The apostle Paul tells us that everything we attain to in being with Christ has one objective. This objective is that "in the coming ages he might show the immeasurable riches of his grace in kindness toward us in Christ Jesus." Ephesians 2:7, RSV. All that God does in us for our salvation He does that our experience might be a witness to others. Our experience is the most powerful evidence we can give in winning others to Christ. But above all, it is a memorial in the coming ages, after sin has been eradicated, that will remind all intelligent beings that God acted in love, mercy, and goodness throughout the great controversy. At the outset of this struggle Satan accused God of being unjust and arbitrary, but when the conflict is over, God will be completely vindicated before the entire universe.

By Grace Through Faith

How is this overcoming experience achieved? Paul declares that it is achieved by grace: "by grace are ye saved through faith." Ephesians 2:8. Grace is God's part; faith is our part. But let us be careful when we say faith is our part, for grace as well as faith comes from God. Note that the same verse goes on to say, "and that not of yourselves: it is the gift of God." The faith we have, we receive as a gift from God.

How can a human being believe, who is dead in trespasses and sins? How can anyone believe whose desires are controlled by sin? How, for instance, can a person believe whose will is captive to lust? How can a person believe whose mental capacity was useless because of his uncontrolled sexual passions? The truth is, he cannot believe. However, God can engender faith in such a life. Faith is a gift of God in the human experience. When a human being receives it, he unites himself with Christ, and God vivifies every faculty which previously was dead.

This is a spiritual resurrection. If physical death results in unconsciousness (see Ecclesiastes 9:5), and resurrection results in restored consciousness (see Isaiah 26:19), something similar takes place in the spiritual realm. The soul that is "dead in trespasses and sins" (Ephesians 2:1), but is spiritually resurrected, possesses a new consciousness. He can now think thoughts that before he was unable to think. What before was to him "foolishness" (1 Corinthians 2:14) becomes "the power of God unto salvation" (Romans 1:16) and is supremely sensible.

This resurrection is not accomplished by human efforts "lest any man should boast." Ephesians 2:9. It cannot be accomplished by unaided good works, because everything we do in this condition is a work of death. It is a work of wrath. It is a work of disobedience. It is a work of the flesh. Everything man does in his natural condition is a work of perdition. We are condemned, totally and completely. Nevertheless, it is marvelous that God, together with Christ, raises us to life. He gives us faith, indispensable for spiritual resurrection. He gives us power, indispensable to live and to witness. Death has no power. Only a living being can act with power. He is mobilized and feels that something is transforming him internally. The internal action of the Spirit is manifest in external actions and in witnessing to others.

Now that we are revitalized, revivified, resurrected, "we are his workmanship, created in Christ Jesus for good works." Ephesians 2:10, RSV. To be with Christ means to experience the new creation. A spiritual creation which causes us to be new creatures. "If any man be in Christ, he is a new creature: old things are passed away; behold, all things are become new." 2 Corinthians 5:17. The "old things" no longer control us. We are made new.

Re-created for Good Works

A new life means completely new. This new life includes the spiritual life, the mental life, and the physical life. The former life-objectives were of the world—disobedience, lust, etc. But now there are new objectives—good works—God working in and through the newborn soul.

An individual that is dead can do nothing to resurrect himself. He cannot work to justify himself. He is unjust. He cannot work to save himself. He is lost in sin. But now that he is resurrected, justified, saved, his works are acceptable to God, because God is working through him. Now a living being works. A just being does works of justice. A saved being lives out his salvation. He has been "created in Christ Jesus unto good works." Ephesians 2:10. Now he is not a son of disobedience, but a son of obedience. Now he is not a child of wrath but a child of mercy. Instead of deserving God's wrath, he deserves His acceptance. Why? Because now he is with Christ.

The person who is with Christ is a new creature, re-created in Christ Jesus for good works, "which God hath before ordained that we should walk in them." Ephesians 2:10. Observe that Christ ordained them, or "prepared [them] beforehand." RSV. Even the works that we do as new creatures, in the final analysis, are in reality the works of God. Now we can glory in something! Saved to constantly and eternally show gratitude to God! In the past we walked with the current in the worldly ways of this age, but now we walk in good works. With the same persistence that we committed sin, we now perform good works. We are now impelled by a mind that has placed itself under God's control. In that way the will, the desires, the thoughts, the mind, all that we are, are completely dedicated to good works; for this is the purpose for which the Lord re-created us.

The spiritually resurrected Christian will not be fainthearted and weak, lacking willpower and the desire to do the works of the Lord. He is a revitalized person, full of power. A Christian cannot keep from doing good. He is with Christ. He lives with Christ. He walks continually with Christ. He lives as a redeemed person.

Through being with Christ, the Christian has a spiritually revived physical life; for the spiritual resurrection he has experienced includes a "resurrection" of the body—a revitalization of his physical being.

In this spiritual-physical resurrection he is freed from those infirmities that have their origin in the mind. According to Ellen White, nine out of ten illnesses originate in the mind. If the Christian is always with Christ and remains with Him, he can have such mental health that 90 per cent of his sicknesses will disappear. (See *Selected Messages,* bk. 2, p. 288.)

Good works include the mental attitude, the customs, the life habits, the entire person. Good works are a product of the power of God acting in us.

The power of God actively manifested itself in resurrecting Christ from the dead and enthroning Him in heaven, and He made us to sit together with Him in heavenly places. That enthronement of Christ in heaven was an act of power. All things were put under His feet in earth and in heaven. Now that we are also enthroned with Christ, power also is granted to us. Not over the things of heaven and earth, but over the powers that before kept us dead in trespasses and sins. Now, re-created in Christ Jesus for good works, we have power to conquer the prince of the power of the air. Now we have power to cease from disobedience. Now we have power to be free from worldliness. Now we have power to control our wills and our thoughts. Now, completely free, totally identified with Christ and fully integrated into His church, we can act in harmony with the will of God. All these things are gifts from God which we receive when we are re-created "unto good works."

Why We Need Reconciliation

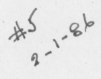

Paul begins the next part of his letter (Ephesians 2:11-22) with the two words "therefore remember." RSV. This means that, as a result of having been re-created, now that you have life from Christ, now that you are living with Christ, now that you are re-created for good works, keep this transformation fresh in your memory. This is Paul's way of introducing the theology of remembering.

The Theology of Remembering

To remember is basic for the Christian. Paul explains this teaching more fully when he talks about the Lord's Supper. See 1 Corinthians 11:22-34. According to the Gospel of Luke, Christ, when He instituted the Communion service, gave the charge, "This do in remembrance of me." Luke 22:19. This remembering is carried out in an act—an important church rite. In partaking of the Lord's Supper we remember Christ. However, among Christians the Communion service should not only be something to remember, but also something *to proclaim*. Paul adds this dimension to the theology of remembering when he says, "As often as you eat this bread and drink the cup, you proclaim the Lord's death until he comes." 1 Corinthians 11:26, RSV.

The remembering starts from the time the service was established and continues until the second coming of Christ. That is the period of hope, the period of Christ in us. See Colossians 1:27. To remember Christ is to have Christ in us. The Lord's Supper symbolically incorporates Christ into the life of the Christian. This is repeated throughout the entire time of hope. Remembering and hoping are united during this period of time until "the glorious appearing of the great God and our Saviour Jesus Christ"—the "blessed hope." Titus 2:13. The Christian who does not remember is in danger of losing hope and ceasing to proclaim Christ.

The apostle Peter also elaborates on the theology of remembering. He says he wrote his two epistles in order to remind his readers. See 2 Peter 3:1, 2.

How does the Christian remember? According to Paul, he remembers by celebrating the Lord's Supper. According to Peter, he remembers by becoming a partaker of the divine nature and through diligence in faith, virtue, knowledge, self-control, steadfastness, godliness, brotherly affection, and love. See 2 Peter 1:3-7, RSV. He who does not have these things loses his spiritual discernment and is "blind and shortsighted and has forgotten." 2 Peter 1:9, RSV.

What must the Christian remember? According to the apostle Peter, he must remember the writings of the prophets (2 Peter 3:2), the commandment of the Lord (2 Peter 3:2), the coming of Christ (2 Pet. 3:4), the creation by the word of God (2 Peter 3:5), and the cleansing of his old sins (2 Peter 1:9).

According to Peter, false teachers say that it is not necessary to keep the Lord's commandments; that Christ has delayed His second coming, and thus it is not necessary to proclaim His imminent return; that the creation did not happen by God's speaking things into existence in six literal days; and that sins are not dealt with according to the procedure explained in the Scriptures. They do not remember.

Besides telling us to remember Christ, Paul, in Ephesians, teaches that we must also remember our past.

The Worthless Past

Paul refers to the past by using such phrases as "in time past" (Ephesians 2:11), and "at that time" (Ephesians 2:12). The deeds in the life of the past, Paul says, were characterized by worldly conduct, disobedience, lust of the flesh, and rebellion. See Ephesians 2:2, 3.

The history of a people comes to light when one studies the meaning of the things they did in the past. All of these activities were important at the time and have significance to the present. Worthless deeds, wasted time, do not build for the future. They are there in the record, but they do not contribute to the historic fame and prestige of a people. Paul tells us that we should remember the past. Not simply to dwell on it, but in order to see the drastic change Christ has wrought in us. The worthless past is empty because it is without Christ, without hope, and without God. It is without enduring meaning. The history of the Christian community does not begin in that past time. It begins with the change brought about by reconciliation.

We should remember our Christless past only to remind ourselves of the change our Saviour has made. When the gospel is preached as a witness, we put far behind us the time when we were without Christ. When we celebrate the Lord's Supper, looking forward with hope to His return, we are separating ourselves from the time we were without hope; and when we live in harmony with the commandments, following the will of God, we are putting at a great distance behind us the time we were without God in this world.

A life of sin is a kind of anti-life. It contributes nothing to the formation of a people. It does not promote true happiness. To the contrary, it divides the community.

According to Paul, the church in Ephesus "in time past" was divided into two groups: some had been afar off and some had been near. See Ephesians 2:17. Those who were far away had a meaningless, worthless past, and even those who were near had not achieved an intimacy with God. At that time they were not together as God's church.

A Distant Proximity

Those who were afar off were the "Gentiles," the "uncircumcision." Ephesians 2:11. They were "aliens from the commonwealth of Israel" (Ephesians 2:12); aliens from the corporate theocratic community; aliens from the life of God (Ephesians 4:18). They were aliens from God because their mental attitude put them at enmity with Him, and alienated them because of their wicked works and practices. See Colossians 1:21. They were "strangers from the covenants of promise." Ephesians 2:12.

The Israelites, or Jews after the flesh, on the other hand, "were nigh." Ephesians 2:17. They were near to God and constituted part of the community of the covenant. Yet, paradoxically, they were as far from God as the Gentiles because they failed to live up to their privileges. They were far from God because of their formalism. The circumcision that they practiced had become a mere form—"made by hands" and "in the flesh." Ephesians 2:11. To really enter the true community of the covenant and be in intimate relationship with God they needed "that circumcision . . . [which is] of the heart" (Romans 2:28, 29), the circumcision of Christ (Colossians 2:11), the circumcision in the spirit (Philippians 3:2, 3).

The Israelites are said to be far from the Gentiles because they are separated by "the middle wall of partition" (Ephesians 2:14) put up by the Jews. This separation is not the separation of the holy from the unholy. Rather, it is the legal system of dogmatic rules that created a separation between Jew and Gentile. Distance and separation among various groups today characterizes a formal religion. It is this separation that produces the indifferent, the neurotics, the liberals, and the fanatics. This separation retards the spiritual edification and building up of the Christian community, the church.

Some are agitated and exasperated by this situation. True, it brings embarrassment, disparagement, and shame. But God is not irritated. He makes the best of our situation by proceeding to work out a reconciliation. In the case of the Ephesians Christ transformed this state of affairs. The Gentiles who were afar off, He brought near. See Ephesians 2:13. The middle wall of partition that separated the Jews from the Gentiles, He broke down. See Ephesians 2:14.

The enemies are now united. There is neither Gentile nor Jew. There is neither far off nor close at hand. There is neither formalist nor liberal. Enmity no longer exists. There are not two, but one. Now there is only the new man—reconciled. See Ephesians 2:15, 16.

The Time of Unity

Christ abolished "the enmity" that existed between Jew and Gentile. He brought the "Good News of peace," and "has made peace between us . . . by making us all one family." Ephesians 2:17, 14, LB.

This unity is not a superficial massing together. It is a unity of transformation. The Jews could not look over nor conceal the middle wall of partition. Neither could they destroy it. Christ Himself must tear it down. No human method can bring together the antagonistic groups and unite them in the church. Craft, diplomacy, or compromise cannot accomplish unity in the church. Christ is the only One who can create it. He can do the same for the church today.

The Gentiles did not need to exchange their uncircumcision for circumcision of the flesh. What they needed was to be spiritually circumcised. Religion made by human hands is totally inadequate. What is needed is a religion made by God. Humanism, with all its implications, must be replaced by spiritual Christianity. Colossians 2:11, 12.

Christ is the only One who can unite the Christian conservative and the Christian liberal. He does so in the same way that He united Gentile and Jew—by reconciliation. Now there is no group afar off made up of Gentile liberals and humanists. Neither is there a group close by composed of formal, conservative Jews. They are all reconciled in One—Christ.

Paul is referring to the then present time—the experience of Jew and Gentile after reconciliation. The apostle puts it this way: "Now in Christ Jesus." Ephesians 2:13. "In Christ Jesus" means "in the church." When Paul concludes the doctrinal section of this epistle, he gives glory to God for His power working in us and then says, "To him be glory in the church and in Christ Jesus." Ephesians 3:21, RSV. Also, in Ephesians 2:16, after he has pointed out that the time is *now*, he says that Christ through the cross reconciled both groups—Jews and Gentiles—unto God "in one body." In his epistle, the references to the body identify it as the church. See Ephesians 1:22, 23.

The church today needs unity. Through the reconciliation, God "hath made both one." Ephesians 2:14. The reconciliation is not simply nearness. It is integration, it is identification, it is unity.

Why do we need reconciliation with God? Because only in this way can we be transformed into sons of God by faith. See Romans 5:1, 10, 11. It is only through this means that the church can become completely unified. The church can achieve unity only if it is made up of new creatures who feel the joy of the new birth and communicate this joy to others.

True unity is the result, not of compromise, but of genuine reconciliation. Reconciliation transforms us into sons and daughters of God—brothers and sisters united together in Christ. A church full of reconciled people is freed from antagonism and conflict. The fanatics stop their disputing, the worldly ones lose their indifference, the liberals renounce their humanism. All become well balanced, understanding, spiritually mature. All live to serve God and His church. All experience the exuberance and vitality of a spiritual resurrection and close relationship with God.

Privileges and Duties

The apostle Paul continues his epistle saying, "Now therefore." In other words, now that you Gentiles, you who were uncircumcised, you who were afar off, you who were aliens. . . ; now that you Jews, you who were formal, you who separated yourselves from others. . . ; now that you fanatics, you worldly ones, you liberals, you conservatives. . . ; now that all of you have been reconciled unto God and live in close relationship with Him. . . ; now that you are not a heterogeneous community of antagonistic groups, but a united church . . . —"now therefore ye are no more strangers and foreigners, but fellowcitizens with the saints, and of the household of God." Ephesians 2:19.

A stranger or foreigner did not have any close ties with a particular city because he did not belong there. The stranger was only passing through. The foreigner was not welcome because he was an "outsider" *(pároikoi).* He might stay longer than the stranger *(xenos),* but neither "belonged." Both were entitled to protection in the city, if they paid a small fee. But once they paid this, they were under no other obligation to the city. They were not citizens. It was different with the Christians in Ephesus. Everyone was a citizen of his new community—the church—enjoying their rights and fulfilling their duties as citizens.

No church member should feel that he only has rights and privileges—the right to freely express his opinion, the right to be heard by others, including the church leaders. Along with his rights, he also has duties and obligations. The Christian maintains and defends the unity of his church. He obeys the authorities as well as protects the doctrinal purity of the church.

Sometimes there are church members who act as if they are not an integral *part* of the body of Christ. They seem to think that they can introduce any idea whatsoever into the body of Christ. They claim they are free and have liberty to do as they please in the church. They forget that the true member of the church has duties as well as rights—obligations as well as privileges.

Once reconciled, we are no longer strangers. We are fellow citizens with the saints. No one in the church, be he great or small, has a right to instigate conflict, whether in conduct or ideolgy. Neither should he express feelings of bitterness, because a Christian has no right to harbor such feelings. The reconciled follower of Christ has a spirit of happiness and fulfills the ministry of reconciliation. As a member of the family of God, he is duty bound to do "good unto all men, especially unto them who are of the household of faith." Galatians 6:10. This household is a family that has a close relationship to God. Every day as the members of this family go about their duties, they perform them as members of the family of God—in unity, in harmony, in association with their heavenly Father. They know that in each activity they represent that family.

An Integral Part of the Structure

According to the Scriptures, no one builds by himself. God is the builder, and He does not build His church with its members isolated from each other. God builds all the members of His family together, each related to each.

There are Christians who claim that religion is a personal matter. This is true. But it is not the whole truth. It is more than a personal matter; it is also a matter that concerns Christians as a whole. Religion is also part of the *ecclesía*. Notice: It is "built upon the foundation of the apostles and prophets, Jesus Christ himself being the chief corner stone; in whom all the building fitly framed together groweth into an holy temple in the Lord: in whom ye also are *builded together* for an habitation of God through the Spirit." Ephesians 2:20-22; emphasis supplied.

If religion and spiritual edification were strictly personal matters, Christ would not have established a church. He would have left each Christian to act individually, separate from the other Christians. But this lack of unity does not reflect the idea Christ had for His church. Disunity in the Bible is symbolic of being separated from God; reunion is symbolic of coming together in Him. God's people are to be a united people. They are not to be fragmented. In the Old Testament, whenever God dispersed His people, He did it as a punishment, and when they repented, He reunited them.

When God does His building and edifying work in a Christian, the influence of that Christian is exercised for good over the rest, and these others also participate in his growth. A true religious experience denotes personal growth and community growth.

How does the church grow? Its growth is similar to that of constructing a building. It proceeds in an orderly fashion. The church is built on the foundation of the apostles and prophets, and Jesus Christ Himself is the cornerstone. A church grows when its spirituality and numbers of born-again believers is increasing. Spiritual growth takes place when church members dedicate time to Bible study, because it contains the teachings of the apostles and prophets, and who, in turn, bear their testimony of Christ. Corporate growth in the church takes place when church members bear their testimony of Christ to others.

The apostle Peter, speaking of the growth of the church, says, "To whom coming, as unto a living stone, disallowed indeed of men, but chosen of God, and precious, ye also, as lively stones, are built up a spiritual house." And he adds, "Ye are a chosen generation, a royal priesthood, an holy nation, a peculiar people; that ye should shew forth the praises of him who hath called you out of darkness into his marvellous light." 1 Peter 2:4, 5, 9.

We as Christians are edified together as we witness to others. Our witness and that of other church members must be consistent. It is God's desire that we be transmitters of His work of salvation, of the gospel of peace, of reconciliation.

In carrying forward the work of reconciliation, we are participating together, not only in the re-creation of the new man, but also in the task that God has entrusted to those who were recently born again. The new man is also to be a witness. He too is entrusted with the ministry of reconciliation. He is not merely to experience peace; he is to bring peace, the gospel of peace, into the lives of others.

This communication of the gospel of peace promotes peace in the church. We cannot pretend to be part of the divine program of the proclamation of the gospel and each go his own separate way in the church program. It is inconsistent for one to claim that he is united with God, while at the same time he undermines the structure of the church. The church is the sum total of all Christians working and living together in harmony with each other. If there is no cooperation and harmony in the church, there is no spiritual vitality in the life of those who profess to belong to the church community. Unless such a spirit is checked, the end result is disintegration, for Christ has said that a house divided against itself cannot stand. See Matthew 12:25. Only when the Christian community is edified together in unity and harmony, demonstrating all the characteristics that pertain to the divine character, can it completely fulfill its function as a witness to the world.

The gospel cannot be proclaimed by proxy. If this were God's plan, the church could amass sufficient funds and contract with a publicity agent to spread the gospel. But this is not God's way of doing things. God's way is to proclaim the gospel through the personal testimony of the members of His church.

The gospel is the communicating of an experience. It is the proclamation of a way of life accomplished, not merely by one's words, but by the way one lives. This was God's purpose when

He established His church. He made us part of a group of people, who not only proclaim reconciliation to others, but who exemplify it among themselves. Christians are to be people who exemplify peace, who know how to live in harmony, who show goodness, who know how to walk in the way of truth. Truth is to be, not just words or mere theory, but an integral part of daily living. But more than this: Not only is truth to be a part of the personal life of each church member, it is also to be a part of the total church community.

The building up of a united church cannot be accomplished when individual members have irreconcilable differences. On the other hand, it is not achieved by the compromise of principle either. It is effected when the spirit of Christ permeates church members. When this happens, the walls of separation that naturally exist among different groups are torn down. This is the only way divisions in the church can be overcome. This is the only way church members can be integrated into a single body with Christ Jesus as its head.

We live in the last days of this earth's history. Now, more than ever before, it is imperative that unity become a real experience in each Christian and in the church as a whole. If there is one thing that the church lacks today, it is the community experience of reconciliation. If all of us, as members of the Christian body, would live in harmony with each other and have an intimate relationship with God, we would be in a far better condition than we are as we bear the testimony of peace and unity to a society that is living in constant conflict. Now, as never before, unity is needed in the church. More than ever before we need each member to feel he is an integral part of the church, part of a group where there are no strangers or foreigners, where each one lives in harmony with his fellow believers as sons and daughters of God, as members of His family. This is a time when church members should cooperate with God and with each other, a time to grow together into God's holy temple. God wants to increase His presence in His church through His Spirit in such a way that the whole earth will be filled with the knowledge of the gospel.

How to Create Unity

#6
2-8-86

Eph 3 : 1 -13

Unity among church members is a necessity. How can it be achieved? Paul has a simple answer: By missionary activity, sinners—pagans and Jews—dispersed and separated from each other throughout the world can be reunited only by Spirit-filled church members working for the salvation of others.

Missionary activity unites because it calls for a close relationship with God, and as a result it establishes close ties between human beings.

This is what Paul explains to the Ephesians at the beginning of chapter 3 of his epistle. This chapter is divided into three parts. (1) The first thirteen verses explain how Paul received the revelation of the universal gospel and how he was commissioned to preach it to everyone. He describes the revelation and the mission in the form of a personal testimony. (2) The next six verses (verses 14-19) present Paul's prayer for those who receive the gospel. (3) Verses 20 and 21 conclude the theological section of the epistle contained in the first three chapters.

Captives of a Mission

(reason)

Paul begins his testimony by saying, "For this cause I Paul." After this phrase comes his testimony, which he draws to a close in verse 13. Then he repeats the phrase "For this cause" and completes his thought by saying, "I bow my knees unto the Father." Then he outlines his prayer.

Paul felt the need to allude to his personal condition. He was a prisoner of Rome awaiting trial before Nero. Even though he was confined to a rented house and was chained to a Roman soldier, he did not primarily consider himself to be a prisoner of the empire. Spiritually speaking, the Roman authorities held no power over him. Another power controlled his will and determined his actions—the power of Christ. It is primarily in this sense that he considered himself a prisoner. He looked upon himself as a "prisoner of Jesus Christ." This "imprisonment" had laid upon him the burden of preaching the gospel to the Gentiles. His imprisonment under the Roman authorities served only as a living illustration of the binding obligation he felt to carry out the commission Christ had laid upon him.

Paul may also have been alluding to another circumstance. Because he had preached in Ephesus (see Acts 19), it is possible that he was a prisoner of the Romans as a result of some of the Ephesians witnessing against him. This conjecture is not purely speculative, because those who accused him of desecrating the temple at Jerusalem knew that Trophimus, who accompanied Paul to the temple, was "an Ephesian." See Acts 21:27-29. If so, Paul was a prisoner in the providence of God because of the Ephesians. See Ephesians 3:1.

The circumstantial reality of Paul's imprisonment in Rome illustrated a permanent reality in his life. Paul was a prisoner of his divine calling. Each Christian must feel this same captivity. We are all captives of this commission. We should not want it any other way. We should act, feel at liberty, and exercise our will in the sphere of this mission alone. Its frontiers are the limits of our total activity.

The passionate dedicating of oneself to this mission produces unity among Christians. The reality of this unity can be seen whenever people make a concerted effort to save someone from danger. We have all seen how human beings act when someone faces imminent death as a result of an accident, a flood, a fire. Those engaged in such work have a feeling of brotherhood as they work together in a common effort to save a life. Such work can in no way be called "legalistic." People engaged in such work are not concerned about making a good impression on God or on other people. Their concern is for someone in desperate need, someone in immediate danger of losing his life. They put themselves in the victim's place and do on his behalf that which they would want to be done to them, were circumstances reversed. In achieving their purpose of rescuing the endangered person, they work together as a unit, with but one goal in mind—the salvation of the person who may lose his life unless they act. The same should be true of our soul-saving activity. Souls all about us are in imminent danger of losing eternal life.

A person has to be a voluntary captive to the idea of mission. It is dynamic. It practices complete self-denial. But this captivity is absorbing and gratifying. It gives meaning to life and to the sacrifice that life daily imposes itself upon every human being. The Christian lives totally separated from the world and at the same time in close connection with it as he senses that he is a prisoner of Christ for the salvation of those who are lost. He lives in a way that is completely different because he has received salvation and finds himself active in this mission.

A Life Under Grace

By grace, God gives salvation (see Ephesians 2:8) and mission (see Ephesians 3:2, 7, 8). Salvation is the foundation of unity, and mission is its cohesive force.

Paul defines grace with two words: *kindness* and *gift*. Ephesians 2:7, 8. God is kind and gives abundantly. Not only does He give material and spiritual blessings, but He also gives Himself in Christ Jesus. A life under grace reflects these characteristics of God.

The true Christian is a channel of kindness and with an extended hand imparts divine gifts. Paul presents to the Ephesians the glory of grace (Ephesians 1:6), the riches of grace (Ephesians 1:7-10), the gifts of grace (Ephesians 4:6-16), and the ministry of grace (Ephesians 3:2-9).

The glory of grace consists of making us "accepted in the beloved." Ephesians 1:6. The love of God surrounds Christ in such a way that His whole character is impregnated with Him. That is why He calls Him the beloved. No sinner can be made acceptable unless he is totally embraced by the love of God. This is an acceptance that God sheds abroad and the sinner feels. When the Christian is living in the acceptance of God, he experiences two things: He is incorporated into the body of Christ, the church, and he actively participates in mission. The union of attitudes and activities is a vital element in the Christian life.

The riches of grace are abundant. See Ephesians 2:7. They provide redemption and forgiveness, wisdom and prudence. See Ephesians 1:7, 8. Through the riches of grace two basic aspects of human life are combined—life's secular activities and life's religious experience. Wisdom and intelligence are indispensable as one carries on the common activities of life. Salvation, redemption, and pardon are indispensable to the life with Christ, begun in this world and extending throughout eternity. God grants all the abundant riches of His grace. These are necessary, not only for our spiritual life, but for our everyday life as well.

In reality, there is no difference between these two aspects of life for the Christian. All his activities hold the same significance when he is the object of the abundant riches of grace. For the Christian it is as religious an activity to work at his job, to carry on a business transaction, or do his tasks at home, as it is to attend church, read his Bible, pray, or preach the gospel.

People who try to divide their activities into secular and religious are living a dual existence. In the daily round of activities they act like any other human being, subject to their passions, their egotism, their envy, their anger—all the attitudes that pertain to the carnal life that excludes grace. But in the church they act like saints. They make a marked distinction between life in the church and life when at work or at home.

Children cannot understand it when parents act one way at home and another way at church. In such cases the fancy clothes of gentleness and kindness are put on only to be seen at church. At home they garb themselves with the Bermuda shorts of discourtesy or, perhaps, the faded and torn blue jeans of violence. This destroys family unity and fills the church with empty formality. The true Christian does not live this dichotomous sort of life. His conduct is consistent and uplifting. He lives under grace in the church, in the home, in his work—wherever he happens to be.

The riches of God's grace are made manifest for a definite purpose. Paul says they are intended to "reunite," to gather together into one all things which are in heaven and which are on earth. See Ephesians 1:10. There is no separation. There are no separated individuals. Individuals are no longer isolated. They are members of a unit. God brings about this unity by bestowing upon fallen humanity the abundant riches of His grace.

The gifts of grace are the ministries the apostle alludes to in Ephesians 4:7-16. These gifts are wrought specifically in the church. Observe that God does not bestow upon His church gifts. He bestows these gifts in people endowed with gifts—prophets, apostles, evangelists, pastors and teachers. God's purpose is to perfect the saints, to edify the church, and to maintain unity by supplying them with these gifts.

The relationship of church members to those who are exercising the gifts of grace in the church must be one of unity, with no distrust, no suspicion, no independent spirit of separation. And the people who receive these gifts of divine grace, those whose mission is to lead the body of Christ toward perfection, must be completely integrated into the membership of the body of Christ through their blameless conduct. Possession of the gift of church leadership does not set a church leader above the laity. The same is true of the other gifts. Before those who have the gift of teaching teach unity of doctrine, they must live that unity. Before those who have the gift of discerning of spirits warn against deceivers, they must shun all deceit, all counterfeits, and error. Before anyone who possesses a gift calls for unity among believers, he should first act in unity with the church.

The life of unity is manifest also in the exercise of the different ministries. There should be no separation between ministers and church members. In the Christian church there should be no such thing as a group of holy men and another group of lay people. All are to be united in their activities. There exists only one body, one Spirit, one hope, one Lord, one faith, one baptism, one God, and the church is one because all have been called to the same "vocation." See Ephesians 4:1-6. The apostle Peter says that all believers are "lively stones" and members of the "holy priesthood" to declare the wonderful deeds of Him who has "called . . . [them] out of darkness into his marvellous light."

Now they are all the "people of God" because they have obtained mercy. See 1 Peter 2:5-10.

The gifts of divine grace manifest themselves in all believers. Therefore, everyone, in complete unity, participates in missionary action.

The ministry of grace comes through revelation and is made manifest through mission (see Ephesians 3:1, 3, 7, 8) and in the edification of the hearers (see Ephesians 4:29). Revelation explains the mystery and mission communicates it. The purpose of the ministry of grace is to accomplish unity in participating in the inheritance, in church membership, and in the promise. See Ephesians 3:6.

The ministry of grace was also manifest so "that in the ages to come he might shew the exceeding riches of his grace in his kindness toward us through Christ Jesus. For by grace are ye saved through faith; and that not of yourselves: it is the gift of God." Ephesians 2:7, 8. God joins Himself with us by means of grace for our salvation. And we are joined to each other with the grace of God "through faith." God, by grace, grants to everybody acceptance, redemption, pardon, wisdom, understanding, the ministries, revelation, and mission, all of which are integrated into one single way of life that does not separate everyday living from the religious activities of life, and all this is accomplished by faith in Christ.

We live by faith. By faith we trust and are trustworthy. By faith we love and are lovable. By faith we show respect and are respectable. By faith we accept and are acceptable.

Faith fills us with confidence. Confidence gives us hope. Hope enables us to endure suffering. We may suffer and weep, but we are never discouraged. We go forward. We may fall, but we get up and keep on going. Faith never wavers. It is not dismayed. It does not show self-pity. It does not dispair. It trusts. It knows that the dark night has bright eyes up there in the firmament. It knows that the dry branch of winter will burst out in the springtime with lovely, silky-petaled blossoms. Faith carries on, bearing hardship just like the brave soldier marches on to victory. Its warmth melts the icy footprints. It gushes up fountains of cool, clear water in the dry desert. It builds bridges over the deep abyss. It heals pain with patience. It fills emptiness with hope. It dissipates anguish with confidence and trust. It goes through the gateway to Calvary. Faith dispels loneliness by the presence of the risen Christ, and a new and living way is opened up when the chilling snow has covered up and obliterated life's pathway.

Faith never separates believers. It unites them. Ideological battles and doctrinal conflicts will come. Misunderstandings among the various administrations will arise. There may be thievery, dishonesty, and bad investments. There may be bitter feeling over the serious mistakes of those leading out. The spirits of honest men may tremble under the harsh criticism of the leaders, but faith never separates and goes its independent way.

Faith never destroys. The church will go through economic crises, it may be faced with the dangers of schism, it may be threatened with calamity and ruin through campaigns of slander; but faith survives.

Faith edifies. It builds up. It understands. It pardons. Out of the ashes it pulls bright embers to start a blazing new fire. From its tears it takes the salt to season the earth. From its weakness it finds the reason to extend its hand to the Almighty Lord of the universe. Faith is an open hand that is filled every moment by grace: it revels in His glory, shares His riches, uses wisely His gifts and fulfills the ministry entrusted to it.

Living the Mission

Paul presents grace as a fountain from which all the gifts of God proceed. The most important gift of all, of course, is Jesus Christ, the minister of grace. Through Him we receive salvation, and with salvation we receive all things—wisdom, Christian life-style, faith, a full life, the unity of the universe, or doctrine, of inheritance, of promise, of the church, and of mission. Mission is a gift from God. See Ephesians 3:8, 9.

If Paul as "less than the least of all saints" received the gift of mission, all the rest of the saints should consider themselves greater than he is. Not greater in holiness, but rather, greater in the acceptance of the missionary gift.

Mission is related to the revelation of the mystery. See Ephe-

4418

sians 3:3. This mystery was not given that we might know about the past, but it was revealed to the apostles and prophets to show that the Gentiles, who were formerly separated from God and His people, could now become heirs, members of the Christian church, partakers of the promise of Christ Jesus.

In order to build up the body of Christ, the church, with people of every nation, needs to fulfill the church's mission.

Mission consists of (1) proclaiming the gospel, and (2) clarifying the ministration of the mystery. God's gift of mission includes both the gospel and its proclamation to the Gentiles. God not only gave the gospel to the church, but He also gave converts to the church. This was the experience of the primitive church. "And the Lord added to the church daily such as should be saved." Acts 2:47. The church does not win new members. It receives them as a gift from God.

Sometimes we meet people who declare that they can't communicate the gospel to others. They excuse themselves by saying they do not have the gift to accomplish this, or by stating that they don't have an adequate preparation, they don't have the right kind of personality, they lack a knowledge of the Scriptures. But those who do this forget that mission is a gift of divine grace.

The gift of missionary action is like the gift of salvation. It is received and becomes real by faith. Mission does not depend on intelligence, ability, or a person's preparation. It depends on his faith. When we move forward in faith, the power of God works, and sinners accept the gospel.

Missionary, Evangelist, and Theologian

According to Paul, mission is carried out by a twofold ministry. First, by proclaiming the gospel to every unbeliever; second, by making that gospel clear and bright to everyone—believer and unbeliever alike. What Paul considered to be a three-phase ministry carried out by each individual, Western Christianity has divided into three classes of workers—missionaries, evangelists, and theologians. According to this latter plan, the missionary takes the gospel to faraway places, the evangelist carries it to unbelievers near at hand, the theologian explains the truths of revelation, adapting them to the people living in his generation.

Generally speaking, such professionals are considered to have specific tasks: They are looked upon as being independent and separate from the laity. Paul does not separate these functions. For him, a person is at once a missionary, an evangelist, and a theologian. Not only this, but according to him a lay person can and must perform these three tasks. All of us, as believers, must proclaim the gospel, and all of us need to make the truth clear to unbelievers and believers alike.

Mission has a specific objective: "That now . . . might be known by the church the manifold wisdom of God." To whom? To the unbelievers, and to "the principalities and powers in heavenly places." Ephesians 3:10.

This testimony also is of benefit to us. "We have boldness and access with confidence by the faith of him." Ephesians 3:12. When we have confidence and trust, it means that we are firm in the faith. Trust creates an atmosphere of unity.

How to Live Love

#7
2-15-82
Eph 3: 14-21

All who have experienced love know that it is a very pleasant experience. However, most humans seem to be more concerned about receiving love than giving it—more interested in being the object of love than a fountain of love. And yet, we all have the feeling deep down that we really should love those about us. How can we show love? How can we live love?

Most people would like to show steadfast, impartial love. A Christian surely desires to show this kind of love. The apostle Paul explains how this can be accomplished in Ephesians 3: 14-21.

What Comes Before Love

Since everything has a cause, love also must have an "antecedent." Paul explains what precedes Christian love in the following words: "For this cause I bow my knees unto the Father." Ephesians 3:14. The precursors of love are prayer and all that is included in the phrase that Paul has expressed here, "For this cause." The apostle includes two things: unity through reconciliation (see Ephesians 2:11-22) and unity through missionary action (see Ephesians 3:1-13).

Before being able to love, it is necessary to be reconciled, to belong to the missionary brotherhood, and to live a life of prayer. This is the second prayer that Paul records in his Epistle to the Ephesians. In the first prayer, as previously mentioned, the apostle asked God to grant the church, to each of its members, the knowledge that brings salvation and generates power, a calling, and an inheritance. By knowledge the apostle means knowledge that incorporates its possessor into the church as a member. In his second prayer Paul beseeches God to bestow upon the church the knowledge of love. Once the believer has received the gospel, and with the gospel has obtained salvation, he also receives love.

But in order to live love one needs to live a life of prayer. Prayer is vital for love to flourish. What kind of prayer? Prayer that is in harmony with the elements that precede it. Prayer that is offered to God in the spirit of true reverence. The prayer that engenders love must harmonize with its antecedents. We have already commented on the need for true prayer. This point needs to be stressed.

For a moment let us imagine that John, an imaginary person who could represent any one of us, wakes up late. He hurries to the kitchen and gulps down his breakfast because he is late for work. His wife fusses at him, "Why do you always have to sleep in? Because you do, you never have time to have worship or to eat a proper breakfast. And not only that, you're going to be late for work!"

This kind of talk really irritates John. He snaps back a curt reply. Hurriedly he drinks a glass of orange juice and then makes a dash for the door, slamming it behind him as he stomps off in a huff.

On his way to work, every minute seems like an eternity. He begins to really worry and exhibit impatience when he finds himself snarled up in heavy traffic. When he finally arrives at work his boss gives him a cold stare. John knows his boss is displeased because he is late for work. His nerves continue to tighten as he begins his day's work. All the while the argument he had with his wife and the grim look from his boss keeps going over and over in his mind.

As he asks himself, he mulls this over, "Why don't they understand? They don't care about my problems. They know I'm a good worker. I'm not late for work all the time. Why do they have to treat me like this?"

All day long everything seems to go wrong for John. Even his lunch gives him indigestion. When he gets home from work, his wife reports that the children have misbehaved and she wants him to punish them. What a hard day!

When John goes to bed, he kneels down to pray. As a Christian, he feels that it is his obligation to do this. After all, he is an active member of the church. He must not forget his religious duties. He begins: "Thank You, Lord, for all the blessings you have given me today. Bless my wife and my children. May they all live in harmony with your will. . . ." John goes on like this to the Amen.

Such a prayer is meaningless because it does not harmonize with what actually happened that day. It is merely a formal recitation. It cannot engender a life of love.

John's prayer makes no sense to him—or to God. He feels frustrated and defeated.

How different would have been his prayer that night if he had been honest with himself and God. He would probably have prayed something like this: "Lord, forgive me, but tonight I really don't feel like praying. Everything went wrong today—the argument with my wife, the way my boss acted, the way I disciplined the children. All these problems I have had have left me completely worn out. I feel awful. This happens to me so many times, Lord, and when I am reminded of it, I get impatient with myself.

"This morning I lost my temper with my wife. Things seemed to go wrong all day long. What shall I do, Lord? I need help. I can't cope with my problems on my own. At the end of the day I don't even feel like talking with You, because I am ashamed of myself. And yet I need You! I can't live without You. Please forgive me for the way I have acted today and help me by Your grace to do better tomorrow, for Jesus sake. Amen."

John then takes his wife in his arms and apologizes to her, and together they resolve to get up mornings early enough so that they can have family worship together and he can still get to work on time. To act and pray in this manner is to act and pray honestly. This is the kind of prayer that God delights to hear—and answer. When we pray in this manner, we are filled with a sense of joy and gratitude. We receive the love of God, and this is multiplied within us. God pardons us and transforms us. We are then enabled to love others.

The Reverence of Love

We must be completely honest with God, for "all things are naked and open to the eyes of Him to whom we must give account." Hebrews 4:13, NKJV. We should pray prayers that honestly reflect what is happening in our lives. At the same time we should also be reverent. The apostle Paul says, "I bow my knees." Ephesians 3:14. Reverence means that we truly recognize our dependence on God and submit to His will. It means that we pray to the Lord about the things we are experiencing in our daily lives. We tell him about the thoughts we think, the things we desire. Not that He doesn't know about these things before we mention them, but speaking of them specifically helps us crystalize our thinking. Reverence includes saying exactly what is happening to us, knowing that God understands and that He can change our weaknesses into strengths.

There is no biblical imperative that demands that we always kneel in prayer in order to show reverence for God. Depending on circumstances, it may be proper to pray while lying in bed or standing on our feet. See Psalm 4:4; 63:6; Mark 11:25. However, it is our privilege and certainly fitting to kneel to pray. More depends on our mental attitude than our physical posture when we pray. The Pharisee and the publican both stood, when they prayed (see Luke 18:11, 13), but God only heard the prayer of the publican, because he had a humble, reverent attitude.

There are times when it is appropriate to pray while standing or walking, while sitting or lying down, or in whatever position we happen to find ourselves. But far more important than our physical attitude is the spirit in which we come to the Lord. It is customary and proper to kneel for the pastoral prayer in a church service, but it is not mandatory under other circumstances. The important thing is to have spiritual reverence. We need honestly to face our problems, for we cannot try to conceal the facts from God as we pray about the things we are experiencing in our lives.

We are not being reverent when we offer hypocritical prayers to God. We cannot go to the Lord with pretended spiritual courtesy. True reverence is not just formal courtesy that we show to others in everyday living—the memorized recitation of an actor. Reverence is the kind of courtesy that springs from deep down inside the soul—something that wells up from the heart.

Reverence in prayer is also expressed in the way we approach God. Paul says that he knelt "unto the Father of our Lord Jesus Christ." He prayed in a correct relationship with God—a relationship of respect, of security, of confidence, of sympathy, of love. But there is something more. When we pray we have to recognize a relationship of obedience to Jesus Christ.

The apostle calls Him Lord. Every time this title appears in the New Testament it implies an attitude of obedience. The Lord is the One who gives the orders, not we. However, this does not mean that ours is the cold relationship of a slave to his master. Rather, it is a familial relationship. It is a relationship to the Father of our Lord Jesus Christ "of whom the whole family in heaven and earth is named" (Ephesians 3:15) to us. We are members of this extensive family. The church is the family of God. It is composed of people here on earth as well as those in heaven. We humans are not the only ones who belong to the church. It is also made up of heavenly beings. The church is made up of the complete family of God throughout the universe.

The reverence that creates love is actually a spiritual attitude, which is made manifest in true prayer by means of a proper relationship with God, which is expressed by loving obedience to Him, because the Christian is an integral part of the complete family of God—His church both in heaven and earth—whose heavenly and earthbound members are closely united into one.

The Spiritual Preparation for Love

In Paul's prayer we can find the spiritual preparation that the Christian needs in order to love. He requests spiritual power and the dwelling of Christ in the believer.

In order to love, the Christian needs divine power—spiritual strength. Paul beseeches God to "grant you, according to the riches of his glory, to be strengthened with might by his Spirit in the inner man." Ephesians 3:16.

Christian love is not like a wilted flower. It is like a plant refreshed by the dews that God grants through the Spirit. This power must pervade our emotions, our reason, our conscience, and our will. We need all these in order to live love, especially so when we are dealing with people who act against us, who appear unworthy of our love. When we live in harmony with God's Spirit, we can love with the love that covers a "multitude of sins." 1 Peter 4:8.

How pleasant it is to know people who show understanding when we do something wrong. Such individuals don't seem to notice the bad side of things. They only speak kind words and demonstrate a helpful attitude. They try to smooth things over and kindly help to correct the mistake. The Christian with spiritual strength looks for the positive side in everything. If someone does him wrong, he responds with understanding and overlooks the defect. This spiritual strength places him in the position to love.

Christ dwelling in the believer is the second spiritual preparation, indispensable to a life that lives love. No passing emotion, it is the result of Christ dwelling permanently in the individual. And how does this happen? By faith. "I am crucified with Christ: nevertheless I live; yet not I, but Christ liveth in me: and the life which I now live in the flesh I live by the faith of the Son of God, who loved me, and gave himself for me." Galatians 2:20.

The dwelling of Christ in the believer is similar to the dwelling of God in the church. Paul compares the church with the building of a holy temple "for an habitation of God through the Spirit." Ephesians 2:21, 22. The indwelling of Christ does not happen in some imaginary unreal way. It comes about by the knowledge of the faith which is closely connected to the doctrines. And it manifests itself in love.

Paul expresses the stability of this type of life by using two illustrations: (1) The imagery of roots growing deep in good soil: We must be rooted and grounded in the faith and "not moved away from the hope of the gospel." Colossians 1:23. (2) The imagery of a building: We must be "stablished" [established] and "built up" in Christ Jesus by faith. Colossians 2:7.

When we accept Christ in our lives, we are contributing to the edification of the church. When we witness for Christ, we are also working for its edification. Both actions result in love. The church is not built up with hate. It is built up with love. The church is not built up with animosity or gossiping. It is not edified with craft or bitter criticism. It is built up with comprehensive, all encompassing love.

If Christ dwells in us, we will always act out of the love motive, in a constructive way. Our goal will be to help build up God's church. The indwelling of Christ by faith permits us to understand the calling, the hope, the proclamation, and the church.

The dwelling of Christ in the believer happens in two ways. One, objectively, "by his Spirit." Ephesians 3:16. The other, subjectively, "by faith." Ephesians 3:17. Thus with spiritual vigor and Christ's presence in us, we are prepared to live a life of love.

The Life of Love

Paul has a reason for praying for spiritual strength and for the indwelling of Christ by faith in the heart of the believer: "That Christ may dwell in your hearts by faith; that ye, being rooted and grounded in love, may be able to comprehend with all saints what is the breadth, and length, and depth, and height; and to know the love of Christ, which passeth knowledge, that ye might be filled with all the fulness of God." Ephesians 3:17-19.

When we possess the unity of reconciliation, when we are an integral part of the missionary community, when we live the prayer life, when we have the fortitude granted by the Holy Spirit, when we have Christ within us, and when we edify the church, we possess the necessary preparation to live a life of love.

The life of love is made steadfast and firm by the exercise of faith. It is "rooted" and "grounded." Here again we see the imagery of the firmly established root in the good soil and the building of an edifice. Christian love has deep roots like a fruitful plant. It has a solid foundation like a well-established building.

Basically the life of love experiences two things: understanding and knowing. When the Christian lives a life of love, he is fully able to comprehend the fullness of love—its width, its length, its depth, and its height. Encompassing the totality of love in a comprehension which surrounds the whole life and being of the believer, he is in a condition to understand and attract all those about him. He empathizes with these people no matter how complicated their problems. He loves them with all the dimensions of love. He attracts them with the magnetic power of love. He makes them part of the same body to which he belongs and, in so doing, contributes to the growth of the church and its unity.

This experience not only makes the believer do good to others, but also it energizes him to accomplish the highest good for them individually. He loves each one with a love that yearns for the individual's salvation, and he cannot rest until that person receives the blessing of salvation in Christ Jesus.

The experience of *knowing* the love of Christ introduces the Christian to the reality of love from an intellectual point of view. If the life-giving comprehension of love places the Christian in contact with the fullness of love, the intellectual knowledge of it makes him know the reality of it. In speaking of this knowledge Paul uses a word that means "effective knowledge"—knowledge actually obtained. This knowledge demands effort. It is not obtained by intuition. It is gained by dedication. This love does not come as a result of emotion; it is the product of intelligent discipline.

On the other hand, this quality of captivating the intellect does not reduce it to the limited sphere of speculation, nor is it clothed in the coldness of rationality. It has to do with a knowing love that "passeth knowledge" (*gnósis*, Ephesians 3:19). It goes beyond that which can be obtained by the sharpest intellect and includes much more than the most developed reasoning powers can attain. It includes the intellectual knowledge of love and the incorporation of its reality.

The love of Christ is not lived by impulse. Its presence in the Christian is complete, real, and enduring. It is not fleeting, subject to the ever-changing things that make up life. During every moment of life in this sinful world, we face a variety of situations. Many times life is burdened down with negative elements, but nothing can alter love. Nothing can change that kind of love. See 1 Corinthians 13:8.

The comprehension of total love and the higher knowledge that embodies the reality of love is not obtained by isolated individuals. It is obtained "with all saints." See Ephesians 3:18. The Christian is not shipwrecked on a lonely island of love. He belongs to a community—the church. The totality and reality of love must be obtained there. The church is the community of love that is active in the world for the salvation of sinners.

The life of love is lived in the following paradoxical, twofold dimension: Within the church and toward the world. The Christian lives in the church in the harmony of that love and projects to the world the gift of its love.

The life of love has one objective. Paul tells the Ephesians that they must love so that they "might be filled with all the fulness of God." Ephesians 3:19. In the same epistle Paul clarifies what he means by the expression "fulness of God." He says that the fullness of God is Christ. And the church is "the fulness of him that filleth all in all." Ephesians 1:23.

Paul concludes his supplication by praying that his readers might all have a life of love, affirming that the Christian's ultimate objective is working for Christ and His church. To have the fullness of God means to be totally accepted by Christ and to be completely incorporated into His church. With this reference to the fulness of God, Paul concludes the doctrinal section of his Epistle to the Ephesians.

In closing, Paul exclaims, "Now to him who is able to do immeasurably more than all we ask or imagine, according to his power that is at work within us, to him be glory in the church and in Christ Jesus throughout all generations, for ever and ever! Amen." Ephesians 3:20, 21, NIV.

Notice all the superlatives that Paul uses here. There is God's superlative power, the super abundance of His gifts to all generations, throughout the superlative time of "for ever and ever!"

Paul is expounding doctrine and giving glimpses of the revelation of God in Christ and the church. The Christian who accepts this doctrine lives in Christ and in the church. He lives a superlative experience in conduct, in unity, in mission, and in love. His life also is superlative. He believes in Christ and has eternal life. Eternal life that begins now. It is by faith that the Christian remains in Christ and in the church for ever.

Christian doctrine is summarized in the supreme power of our God, who is at work bestowing a super-abundant salvation to all generations throughout all ages. For this salvation we glorify God in Christ, in the church.

How to Live One's Vocation

Paul was a prisoner. He begins the second part of his epistle by alluding to this disagreeable situation in his life. Deprived of his liberty, but not of his surety in God, he writes about the Christian's vocation. See Ephesians 4:1-16.

Even though he does not separate practical living from the matter of doctrine or vice versa—they are always interrelated—he emphasizes, as we have noted, doctrine in the first portion of his epistle and conduct in the latter. Now as Paul writes concerning Christian living, he prays for their conduct. "I . . . beseech you that ye walk." By to "walk" Paul means Christian living. To walk in the ways of the Lord means to live in harmony with the will of God. This concept is found in a number of places in the Bible. Paul appeals for Christians to live, to conduct themselves, worthy "of the vocation." Verse 1.

If there is a worthy way to live a calling, we can conclude there must be an unworthy way as well. Paul makes an interesting play on the Greek word *ekklesia*, translated "church," and literally meaning, "called out." The apostle refers to the *church* in the foregoing verse, Ephesians 3:21. This, therefore, is the antecedent of the words *"vocation" (klēseos)* and *"calling" (eklēthēte)*. Verses 1, 4. These three words are from the same Greek root. The church is the assembly of the called ones—those who are called.

One lives his vocation in relationship to the church—its mission, its doctrine, and its growth. Living one's vocation is also seen in one's personal conduct as a Christian—in his humility, his meekness, and his patience.

Paul describes the life of the Christian and the church in the following chapters. Chapter 4 emphasizes patience, humility, unity with the entire body of believers, unity of doctrine, and unity in the growth of the church. In the first part of chapter 5 he explains the moral behavior of those who accept this vocation; then he refers to life in the home. See Ephesians 5:21-33; 6:1-9. He closes the second part of his epistle explaining the victorious life. See Ephesians 6:10-20.

The Life Worthy of the Calling

First, Paul describes *humility* as one of the characteristics of the life worthy of the calling. In order to live up to our calling, we must be humble. Paul says that we must live in "all [not partial] lowliness" (Ephesians 4:2); in other words, humility. What then, is humility? It is the opposite of pride. What Paul is really saying is, "From now on, in answer to your calling, you must live without pride."

How is it with our lives? Is there any pride lurking there? Have we ever said, "I'm going to show that person who I am!" Such an attitude comes from pride.

Sooner or later pride causes suffering. The greater the pride, the greater the suffering. Most of us feel bad when we discover that someone has been gossiping about us. Why? Because our pride is hurt. The person who spoke ill of us did not so much as touch us, yet we felt hurt because our pride was wounded.

Christ suffered when He was here on earth. However, He suffered, not because of pride, but because He vicariously bore the sins of the human race—your sins and mine.

Paul tells us that we must have a life of complete humility without the least vestige of pride. Interestingly, true humility does not cause self-depreciation. It does not destroy our personal worth. We value ourselves in the light of the price paid on Calvary for our redemption. Our life is one of dignity, not of self-flagelation. We do not live in a neurotic state that plunges us into an abyss of inferiority complexes. True humility recognizes the value that Christ's sacrifice placed upon each one of us. Our worth is equal to the total value of Christ's life and this value is immeasurable.

He gave His life to save us. Humility hides itself, sustains itself, and values itself in Christ Jesus.

Have you ever seen a counterfeit twenty-dollar bill? Sometimes it is almost impossible to distinguish a counterfeit bill from a genuine one. To the untrained eye they may look identical, but there is an essential difference—one was printed by the U. S. government, the other was not. They may give every appearance of being the same, but one is genuine, the other is a counterfeit. It is false.

The difference between dignity and pride may seem undiscernible, but there is an essential difference. True Christian dignity bears the impress of Christ's character; pride bears the stamp of the antichrist.

The humble life is a life built up by Christ. It reaches its full height through the vocation or life-style to which he has called us.

The second element Paul discusses in the life worthy of God's calling is *meekness*. The apostle Paul introduces the social aspect of Christian conduct when he mentions this characteristic. Meekness, or gentleness, helps to build up those about us because it is nonviolent and thus non-destructive.

There are people who become offended because the church nominating committee did not ask them to serve in a certain position. They are offended by the decisions of the church leaders whom they believe to be in error. They form a group of malcontents to express their dissatisfaction. Their goals and objectives may appear to be holy and good, but they act with "violence." This is not worthy of the Christian calling. Only meekness is worthy of such a calling.

Some professed members of Christ's body demonstrate a lack of meekness in another way. They see injustices, either real or imagined, and either within or without the church, and, disregarding the counsel of James 5:1-8, they take it upon themselves to right these wrongs. Frequently, they use violent methods to carry out their apparently good ideas. But a truly good cause does not engender the spirit of violence. Violence exists when there is an absence of meekness.

Others exhibit a lack of meekness another way. They become captivated by a certain doctrine and give it their private interpretation. They talk about the matter on every occasion and to anyone who will listen. They magnify the importance of this particular teaching under the lens of their own private interpretation and condemn anyone who fails to see matters as they see it. Frequently such persons pass judgment on the church and insist that it is in error because it does not see their hobbyhorse in the same light they do. Beneath this seeming zeal for "truth" one will usually discover, sooner or later, a lack of meekness, and yet violence is its ultimate result, for it brings dissension into the church.

All of us have probably seen cases similar to those mentioned above, and ideally it has never included us. The spirit of rebellion and lack of meekness will not be found in the life of a Christian worthy of his calling. Only meekness and gentleness will be evident there.

The third characteristic of the life worthy of the Christian's vocation is *patience*. Paul says, "with patience, forbearing one another in love." Ephesians 4:2, RSV.

Patience is the opposite of irritability. Patience helps us to live the Christian life when we are buffeted with afflictions and suffering. James says, "Take, my brethren, the prophets, who have spoken in the name of the Lord, for an example of suffering affliction, and of patience. Behold, we count them happy which endure. Ye have heard of the patience of Job, and have seen the end [i.e., purpose] of the Lord; that the Lord is very pitiful, and of tender mercy." James 5:10, 11.

Patience confirms us in the hope (Romans 15:4), and it helps us to support our brethren, maintaining the unity of the Christian church (Ephesians 4:3). We need patience to run the Christian race (Hebrews 12:1), to inherit the promises (Hebrews 6:11, 12; 10:36), and to develop godliness (2 Peter 1:6).

The Unity of the Spirit

Besides humility, meekness, and patience, the life worthy of the Christian's calling demands *unity*. Paul encourages us to "make every effort to keep the unity of the Spirit through the bond of peace." Ephesians 4:3, NIV.

As we have noted, the apostle also speaks of unity in the doctrinal section of the epistle. He referred to the church as a body, with all the believers being its members. If the body is to remain alive, it cannot be dissected, its parts separated. In the early Christian church the Gentiles and the Jews were united as fellow citizens, as members of the same family, built together into one single church structure. See Ephesians 2:14-22. From corporate unity Paul now passes on to the matter of spiritual unity. He here refers to the total unity of the church.

This unity is based on the existence of one body, one Spirit, one hope, one Lord, one faith, one baptism, and one God. See Ephesians 4:4-6. Paul says that the believer will be anxious to maintain that unity of the church which is already in existence— that unity which already exists is the structural or *corporal unity.* The church's organization in all its forms is maintained by the positive attitude of each believer. That attitude is guided by the Holy Spirit. Corporate unity can only exist when there is spiritual unity.

The believer who refuses to maintain *spiritual unity* in the church becomes alienated from it. His name may still be on the church books—part of the corporate unity—but if the fruits borne by his life make it evident that he is spiritually against the church, he is, in reality, separated from it. Paul urges, in fact he commands the believers, to bend all their emotions, all their sentiments, all their spiritual values to the accomplishment of total unity of the church, both corporate and spiritual.

Unity of Doctrine

With the total unity of the church now established, Paul explains how *doctrinal* unity can be achieved (see Ephesians 4:7-13) and how the church grows in unity (see Ephesians 4:15, 16).

Before "we all come in the unity of the faith, and of the knowledge of the Son of God" (Ephesians 4:13)—i.e., the unity of doctrine—we must first of all have the gifts. Christ "gave gifts unto men" (Ephesians 4:8). It is interesting to note that He gave gifts to men and He gave men with gifts to the church. He calls those men who received the gifts evangelists, apostles, prophets, and pastor-teachers.

In these last days a strange idea is being expounded. Some are saying that the church can live in unity and at the same time have different doctrines. They state that it is more important to preserve unity than it is to preserve doctrines, even fundamental ones. Those who advocate this view assert that one person can have one opinion, another person, another opinion, no matter how inharmonious these might be. The important thing, they say, is to maintain unity. If what one thinks about a certain doctrine is not the same which another believes it to be, that does not matter. The important thing is unity for the sake of unity.

The apostle Paul does not agree with this view. He declares that there is diversity of gifts, but unity of doctrine. But why should there be diversity of gifts? Paul answers: (1) to edify the body of Christ (see Ephesians 4:12) and (2) to maintain unity of doctrine (see Ephesians 4:13-15).

Paul says that we must not be carried about with every wind of doctrine, pointing out that the Lord gave spiritual gifts to the church, that they might be used to maintain unity of doctrine. There is only one true doctrine of any fundamental scriptural teaching. Church members are not at liberty to differ on the distinctive teachings of the church. They must hold the same opinion when it comes to basic truths. If that were not so, where would the veracity of truth be? If for one person the truth is one thing, and for another, it is something else entirely different, which one is truth?

Truth is always the same, because it comes from God and in Him there is "no variableness, neither shadow of turning." James 1:17.

A life worthy of the Christian vocation is a life of doctrinal harmony and unity. When doctrinal conflicts arise over basic tenets of faith, they are wrong, if they destroy unity. If there are differences of opinion over questions of prophetic interpretation, or matters that have no bearing on salvation, or the distinctive teachings of the church, they should be laid aside, if church leaders and men of experience see no light in them.

God gave diversity of gifts so that the church might maintain unity of doctrine and so that its members might be of service to the church. We receive gifts for the perfection of the saints, for the work of the ministry, for the edification of the body of Christ—gifts that we must not use for our own personal exaltation. The exercise of these gifts must honor Christ and His church, for only in this way will we be honored by God and endeared to the Christian community.

Some people aspire to worldly fame and use their God-given gifts to achieve it. But why aspire to fame? Even though someone achieves world renown, with all its supposed benefits, what does it profit a person, if he loses his eternal salvation? See Mark 8:36.

Now let us look at it from the Christian viewpoint. What does a member of Christ's body get out of using his God-given gifts to the glory of God and the benefit of His church? When we properly conduct ourselves in the church, when we live up to our vocation, we have the affection of those in our sphere of action. There is no greater satisfaction than experiencing the love of those who, together with us, are using their gifts for the cause of the church. There is no greater joy than being united with one's brethren in the church who are preaching the same gospel of salvation for lost souls to the glory of God.

Unity of Growth

As we use the gifts that God has bestowed upon us, we will work toward seeing the church grow and flourish. If we fail to do this, the church will eventually lose us along with our gifts. When this happens, God fills the vacancy by supplying others who possess His gifts and who are willing to use them to His glory in the preaching of the gospel.

The early Christian church needed a man to preach the gospel of salvation to the Gentiles. God found him while he was on his way to Damascus to persecute the church. It seems paradoxical, but God had given Paul gifts to be used exclusively for the church. If Paul had not used his gifts for the perfection of the church, today we would know nothing about Saul of Tarsus.

Paul refers to unity in the growth of the church in these words: "Speaking the truth in love, we are to grow up in every way into him who is the head, into Christ, from whom the whole body, joined and knit together by every joint with which it is supplied, when each part is working properly, makes bodily growth and upbuilds itself in love." Ephesians 4:15, 16, RSV.

Paul describes the church as growing in two ways: (1) spiritually, and (2) corporately. The first concerns the members of the church as individuals. The second, the church as an institution. The sum of the two constitutes the true growth of the church.

The spiritual growth of the Christian is not purely subjective. It is not necessarily the intense emotions that some feel on special occasions. It is an objective knowledge—solid, real, based on the truth and in Christ. To attain it, the Christian must follow the truth in love. His bond with truth is not speculative. It is ethical and communal. The objective elements of truth should induce him to lead a moral life of obedience and to be of service to the community. He obeys God's commands and serves His church.

The Christian's growth is in Christ. It is not some kind of imaginary growth; it is a real growth. This growth is well balanced. It "grow[s] up in every way." It is growth in humility and takes place by being in Him who is the head. See Ephesians 4:15, RSV.

Corporate growth refers to the increase of members in the church, and this results in the increase in the number of congregations. This growth of the body produces unity. It is a solid, active growth. The members work together with a common interest; they help one another, and each carries on his activity with complete dedication.

According to the apostle Paul church unity is evidenced corporately, spiritually, doctrinally, and in the manner of its growth. See Ephesians 2:14-22; 3:6; 4:3-16. The Christian vocation and the life worthy of that vocation are linked together with unity.

The Christian life is described with such words as *vocation, call, gifts, talents, service, giving of oneself,* and *church*. The character of a Christian is defined with words such as *humble, gentle, patient,* and *loving*. Such a Christian is active in church endeavors and preserves its unity. The ethics governing the life worthy of the vocation are clearly defined by the Holy Spirit who is sent to maintain the unity of the church in the bonds of peace. It is the intention of God the Father, that through the bestowal of His gifts upon the believer, he is ordained to living a life for the church and maintaining unity in doctrine. This unity is confirmed by Christ, the Head of the church, who declares that constant spiritual and corporate growth is necessary.

The Christian's vocation is lived with dignity, in humility, gentleness, and patience. It is lived in spiritual and doctrinal unity, and there is unity in its growth. This results in peace, perfection, and security.

How to Be Spiritually Renewed

#9
3-1-86
Eph 4: 17-32

Paul refers to spiritual renewal by contrasting two ways of life. One is the way of the Gentiles; the other is the Christian way. The first is the life-style of the "old man," the second, the "new man." See Ephesians 4:17-32. Having described these two kinds of life, the apostle Paul explains how the transformation takes place from the old to the new man. See Ephesians 4:20-24.

In this chapter we shall take a look at the old man and his life of folly and see how this can be changed into the life of the new man.

A Life of Mental Emptiness

Paul describes the sinful way of life only as a means to warn against pursuing such a course. He explains some of its features so that we will clearly understand what he is talking about.

He speaks in no uncertain terms: "So I tell you this, and insist on it in the Lord." Ephesians 4:17, NIV. The apostle is speaking emphatically because he has stated that Christians should live "worthy of the vocation." Ephesians 4:1. This is why they can now be in a position to accept his charge, when he says, "Walk not as other Gentiles walk, in the vanity of their mind." Ephesians 4:17.

Vanity of mind signifies a mental emptiness, a mental void, a state of having no objective or purpose in life. It goes without saying that the mental processes in a living person, irrespective of whether or not he had been born again, never cease altogether.

75 *NIV*
" futility of their
thinking "

However, although the unbeliever thinks, but he is incapable of thinking the thoughts that a Christian thinks; "for they are foolishness unto him." 1 Corinthians 2:14.

The vain, empty mind wastes its time trying to find an explanation for everything. It finds all kinds of arguments, obvious reasons, fictitious knowledge, fantasies of all kinds, but it never comes to a clear comprehension of truth. On the contrary, when it catches faint glimmers of imperfect knowledge, it becomes all the more darkened, deformed, and skeptical.

From the Christian perspective the person with a "natural" mind spends his life on meaningless things. See Romans 1:21, 22. Every little thing, every experience, makes him all the more frustrated. The sophisticated social atmosphere to which he is attracted is only a mirage. Many members of our society are reaching out for what they believe to be the real thing, but when they get close up, the apparent reality of life disappears. Their happiness is but a fantasy. Their realizations are but a dream. No one has achieved a thing.

Life seems to be one great illusion. But these people with "natural" minds have an inner urge that keeps them searching and longing for something that is not there. The "natural" mind cannot offer any real purpose for life. It just can't find any.

When the person in this condition realizes he has been deceived, he becomes frustrated, he rebels, he alienates himself. His turning to drugs, or other vicious habits, is the result of his alienation. He wants to find some sort of satisfying experience. But he doesn't find it. After a while he discovers that drugs, alcohol, and his other indulgences offer him nothing. He continues on in a spiritual vacuum. He loses his physical strength. Eventually his health goes. When he gets sick, he has reached the climax of his meaningless life. In this state of wretched disillusionment, he is overcome with hopeless despair.

The Life of the Enemy Mind

When the apostle Paul explains to the Colossians this type of life, he defines it as a condition of mental hostility (Colossians 1:21, RSV), or having an enemy mind. Says he, "And you, that

N I V "enemies in your minds"

were sometime alienated and enemies in your mind by wicked works, yet now hath he reconciled." Colossians 1:21. The empty mind easily becomes an enemy mind. First, it is at enmity with God, and then hostile to everybody and everything.

The enemy mind is opposed to everything. It is contentious, rebellious, violent. This type of mind is characteristic of life in our time. It was also characteristic of the antediluvians. In those days the land was "filled with violence" (Genesis 6:11)—social violence. The social discontent of the people who had an enemy mind produced a chaotic state of society. It is the same today.

Such a society has a difficult time maintaining itself. It is based on a "natural" mind, and its activities are the product of an enemy mind. It is headed for self-destruction because it has no goals and it is full of violence. Christians cannot live this way, and Paul solemnly charges them not to try to.

But many times professed Christians act as though they had an enemy mind. This is seen in their relationship with one another. Sometimes they are angry, revengeful, and quarrelsome. This reveals they have characteristics of an enemy mind. A Christian should be a friend, not an enemy. Friends do not quarrel or rebel.

The Life of the Darkened Mind

The empty, enemy mind does not have the ability to discover truth because it has a "darkened" understanding. See Ephesians 4:18. It is in darkness when it comes to comprehending the meaning of things. Under these conditions there is the irresistible tendency to distort truth. The darkened mind finds it easy to claim that it alone has the correct view on a matter.

In God's church the Holy Spirit is not active with just one individual to reveal truth. He works through many. When the Holy Spirit reveals something to one individual, He will give the others the capacity to understand the revelation when it is explained to them.

Christians need to be on their guard in this matter. They must be careful not to allow the ignorance that comes from the mistaken or darkened understanding to mislead them, whether it be in their manner of thinking or living, for such ignorance is nothing but the "old man" with his empty, enemy mind, who has his understanding darkened and who is, therefore, incapable of comprehending what the life of God means.

Alienated From the Life of God

Paul goes one step further in explaining the way of life Christians should avoid. He says that those who walk in the vanity of their minds are "alienated from the life of God through the ignorance that is in them, because of the blindness (margin: "hardness" in some Bibles) of their hearts." Ephesians 4:18. To be "alienated" means to be "estranged," and in the context in which Paul uses it, "to have no part in the life of God."

In Old Testament times God established a life of communion with the people of Israel. He confirmed this relationship with a covenant. Because of this covenant, the descendants of Abraham became God's people. They received promises, hope, and God was with them in the world. The "old man" could not partake of this. He did not belong to the covenant. In the past the Gentile Ephesians had lived after the manner of the "old man." At that time they were "without Christ, being aliens from the commonwealth of Israel, and strangers from the covenants of promise, having no hope, and without God in the world." Ephesians 2:12. They lived without belonging to God's community.

It is true that pagans belong to a society. So do unbelievers. All human beings live in a social atmosphere. But they do not, therefore, belong to God's community. They are individualists. From the spiritual viewpoint, they are isolated, independent, socially abandoned. It sometimes happens that they do not even belong to a family. Their family is divided, their parents divorced, their brothers and sisters scattered. It is a life in a society without experiencing social life. And besides all this, they are alienated from the life of God and His community.

In this social alienation, unbelievers experience a psychological alienation. It is not insanity. It is a state of being without identity. Psychologically they are disintegrated because of sin. See Romans 7:15-17.

Sin causes psychological alienation—a life of loneliness. A

loneliness that hurts. This is the loneliness of people who are spiritually empty. They experience everything that alienates one from the life of God. This is especially true of those who once have been in contact with God, who once belonged to Him and have experienced the joy of His life. They cannot help but have a longing for that life again. Perhaps they do not fully realize what it is that they lack. But the anguishing sense of loneliness tells them that they need something else. What they really need is to return to the life of God. How can they do this? By turning to God in faith.

When faith is exercised, it fills the emptiness in the mind. It brings peace to the rebellious mind. It illumines the darkened understanding. It gives identity to the one who has been alienated and incorporates him into the life of God. Why? Because faith accepts the sacrifice and death of Christ as the all sufficient substitute for all his deficiencies. See Galatians 2:20.

One who does not accept Christ by faith keeps on in his old way of life, in a life-style that does not befit the Christian. His is an existence with an empty mind. He has the attitude of an enemy mind, gropes in the errors of a darkened mind, is alienated from the life of God. This situation becomes even more complicated when he gets to the state where he has lost all feeling.

A Life Past Feeling

"Having lost all sensitivity, they have given themselves over to sensuality so as to indulge in every kind of impurity." Ephesians 4:19, NIV. This life "past feeling" (KJV), this insensibility, is a consequence of being separated from God. This separation is caused by ignorance and hardness of heart.

Ignorance frequently is caused by lack of interest. In such instances no effort is put forth to get acquainted with God. There is no desire to do so. Although God makes every effort to reveal Himself to such people, they leave Him out completely. The negligent Christian who does not study the Word of God is on the road to insensitivity and lack of feeling. But a Christian must not let this happen. The apostle ordains that this tendency should be resisted. Many by their lack of dedication and interest, by their negligence of Bible study, allow themselves to drift back into the way of life that they should have permanently left behind.

Paul describes the heart of those who are unacquainted with God as "petrified," when he refers to the hardness of heart (Ephesians 4:18) which causes alienation from the life of God. He uses the word *pōrōsis*—a stone harder than marble. Ephesians 4:18. When this term is used in medicine it applies to the hardening of the arteries, a condition that can end in sudden death. It is also used to express the loss of all capactiy for feeling.

The loss of one's sensibilities affects the entire life. An insensitive person is rude, discourteous, disagreeable, violent, self-centered. He does not care how other people feel or how he makes them feel. It doesn't bother him in the least if he offends someone or makes someone angry. He has no regard for others. The only one that matters is himself. Others have to grovel at his feet. He overshadows them. Everyone must be subservient to him— machines starting and stopping at his every whim. The insensitive person is a quasi-human monster. Frequently such persons are impure, full of lust. He who is lascivious (*aselgeia*, Ephesians 4:19) shows no consideration whatever for public opinion, which only serves to provoke him to further lasciviousness. In this state of indifference, he expresses the basest feelings of human nature— fornication, inordinate affection, evil concupiscence, covetousness, anger, wrath, malice, blasphemy—coupled "with greediness" (Ephesians 4:19), "for which things' sake the wrath of God cometh on the children of disobedience." See Colossians 3:5-8.

Greediness is an arrogant insatiability, an inordinate craving to possess something, an illicit desire to get what belongs to another, a debased spirit that causes a person to sacrifice his neighbor's interests for his own benefit. Greediness is the irrepressible desire to posses that which we have no right whatever to possess.

When Paul beseeches the Ephesians to refrain from that kind of life, he approaches the subject, as he does every other matter throughout the entire epistle, in the context of the church. In this setting we can see the contrast. We then understand that the aimlessness of the empty mind is to be supplanted by the true objective, the missionary zeal of the church; the true light for the darkened understanding is the light of the gospel; the true incorporation into the life of God for those who are aliens is their incorporation into the church; the true sensibility for those who have lost all their feeling and sensitivity is that which proceeds from Christ and contributes to the unity of His own body, the church.

Spiritual Transformation

When an individual forsakes the life-style of the "old man"—of the Gentile, the pagan, the unbeliever—he needs to go through the experience of a true spiritual transformation. This transformation takes place in two spheres, one centered in Christ, the other in the person himself.

Let us notice the three experiences Paul mentions which are centered in Christ. They are, "to learn Christ." We are to hear Him, and we are to be taught by Him. See Ephesians 4:20, 21.

"To learn Christ" means to fill the mind with Him. The New International Version renders the phrase, "come to know Christ." If an empty, aimless mind receives Christ, it receives Him in totality or not at all. The mind that was empty now receives what it has lacked, Christ in His fullness. The total Christ includes the Head and the body, the Saviour and the church. He who receives Christ in his totality has a full mind. He now has worthy objectives—living the Christian life, living a life in the church. He actively participates in the preaching of the gospel and knows that as he is going about his ordinary, daily activities, his actions identify him with the Lord's redeeming acts. Everything he does, he does with reference to Christ, in unity with Him, living as Christ lived, fulfilling the mission of the church. In this sense, his mind is full.

Not only must the individual have Christ as his goal, his ideal, not only must he have Him as an integral part of his thoughts, but he must have something else. Paul says, "if so be that ye have heard him." Ephesians 4:21. *He must hear Christ.* He must have the capacity to listen to Him. The verb "to hear" in the Bible means much more than simply passing through the ears and into the brain. Hearing is equivalent to obeying. For example, implicit in the child Samuel's statement, "Speak; for thy servant heareth" (1 Samuel 3:10), is the idea of obeying what he was to hear.

The whole philosophy of the Bible can be contrasted with Greek philosophy by two words, *hearing* and *seeing*. The Greek sees things. He stands back and objectively looks at things, observes them, and takes note of the various phenomena. He sees how things happen and then tells what he has observed. The Greek considers knowledge to be primarily visual information. His is a scientific knowledge.

Using the scientific approach, one looks, observes, takes note of things, and then draws his conclusions. Information is conveyed about a phenomenon; data is gathered concerning it, and an interpretation is given on the basis of these observations. This process does not necessarily result in the acquisition of true knowledge, but frequently it is confused with it. It is like confusing a beautiful package with the gift inside. To all appearances it is an inseparable unit, and especially so if the package is wrapped in pretty paper and has a nice bow.

Western science has been developed using the same postulates as the Greek used. It is supposedly objective. But in explaining it, the content frequently is confused with the philosophy that puts it all together. The interpretation and the scientific data appear to be one and the same thing.

Hebrew thinking, which is the underlying trend of thought in the Bible, explains man's experiences with the things about him and his experiences with God, by using the verb "to hear." The Hebrew hears the word of Jehovah who created the heavens and the earth. This is neither a physiological nor a psychological hearing. It is ethical. The Hebrew's relationship with God and things is not objective but subjective. He is incorporated into what God says and becomes part of the things made by His word. He himself was created by God. He is totally integrated with Him. He obeys Him.

The wisdom of the Greek mentality and consequently of the entire Western culture, which follows this thought pattern, is prone to manipulating phenomenal evidence, and resists being changed by the data. On the other hand, the true Christian, governed by biblical Hebrew thought, is incorporated into the contents of the Word of God and allows himself to be transformed by it. His attitude is not exclusively objective, as is the Greek; it is also subjective. It includes his very own person. He himself is incorporated into the religious phenomenon. He does not interpret the realities of nature with a philosophy of his own. He interprets them in the light of the Word of God.

We allow ourselves to be taught by Christ. With the true Christian Christ becomes such an integral part of his thought that he willingly obeys Him. When we come to this point, it is not difficult to allow ourselves to be taught by Him. We need this experience in an age when there are so many who disobey Him. It seems so easy to disregard the demands of our religion, to ignore the church and the part it has to play in our lives—to fail to recognize its authority. Why? Because to do the opposite means that we must obey. In these days it is popular to be individualistic. People don't want Christ to teach them. The demands of obedience are offensive. Each one believes he has the right to his own liberty, and he ignores the fact that this right, when exercised independently, shows that he is living the life of the "old man."

The people of God will know the way of obedience because they belong to Christ; they are the people of the revelation, the people of the law, the people of hope, and mission, the people of present truth. Where are the people of obedience? The time has come when we must return to the principles revealed in Holy Writ, when the Word of God, His revelation, is respected, and when the commandments pronounced by the Omnipotent One are obeyed.

For the spiritual transformation to take place, in addition to learning Christ, hearing Christ, and being taught by Christ, there is another sphere of action centered in ourselves. The apostle Paul tells us to divest ourselves of the old man, renew our thoughts, and put on the new man. See Ephesians 4:22-24.

The empty, vain, enemy, aimless mind, must be renewed. It has to pursue a different way of thinking. Paul says, "Be not conformed to this world: but be ye transformed by the *renewing of your mind,* that ye may prove what is that good, and acceptable, and perfect, will of God." Romans 12:2, emphasis supplied. When our minds are renewed, we discover that the will of God is good, acceptable, and perfect. We do not act contrary to the divine will. As the transformation of the mind takes place, we discover that the will of God is not difficult to follow. "His commandments are not grievous." 1 John 5:3. It does not destroy our individuality. It does not deprive us of our liberty. To the contrary, it is good, acceptable, and perfect. It allows us to experience a good life, an acceptable life, a perfect life. Such a mind begins to understand things in a different way. It sees things from God's perspective and causes us to act accordingly.

The person with a renewed mind is not dominated by the humanistic, rebellious, pseudoscientific culture that permeates the world. He doesn't think along ordinary lines any more. He doesn't need scientific proof for religion. He applies the test of faith. He does not require that the revelation of God be explained by history, sociology, psychology, or any of the other disciplines, which the culture in which he lives requires. He studies to find how scripture explains scripture. He understands that the things of God can be understood only by thinking His thoughts. He knows that revelation belongs to the Holy Spirit and that the proof of the revelation comes from the same Source. This does not mean that he is ignorant or depreciates readily available information. He is acquainted with the sciences and with the philosophies that explain human science, and he knows the methods that are applied in these disciplines. But he keeps them in proper perspective. He knows the rules that are followed in the game of life in this sinful world and uses such information carefully. He never underestimates it, but he does not let it become the means for measuring the things of God. His mind is renewed by his new manner of thinking. He is spiritual. His mind transcends earthly limits. He is humble and obedient to God.

With a renewed mind, the born-again Christian follows the counsel of the apostle: "*Put on the new man,* which after God is created in righteousness and true holiness." Ephesians 4:24, emphasis supplied. The new man is a creation of Christ. This new being lives worthy of his vocation, in justice, in holiness, and in truth.

How to Live the Life of the New Man

The new man is a creation of God. God created the first man in His image and likeness. See Genesis 1:26. When sin entered this world, this similarity was destroyed. From that moment on he ceased to be an authentic likeness of his Maker. Sinful man does not represent original man created in the image of God.

So that man might once again bear the authentic likeness of the God who created him, he needs to be re-created. He needs to be, not re-made in the image of his earthly progenitor, but in the image of his heavenly Creator. See 1 Corinthians 15:49.

The re-creation of man in the image of God, not only refers to his form of being, but more important, his character and conduct. His code of ethics includes treating all people alike; being holy; showing love, mercy, kindness, meekness, and patience; forgiving his fellow man; and experiencing the peace of God. See Colossians 3:11-15.

In the Epistle to the Ephesians, Paul points out some of the elements that govern the moral principles of the new man. He speaks the truth, he does not practice sin, he works and gives of his bounties to others, he speaks what is edifying and good, and he forgives as God forgives. See Ephesians 4:25-32.

Speaking the Truth

Paul speaks of honesty when he is describes the life of the new man. "Wherefore putting away lying, speak every man truth with his neighbour: for we are members one of another." Ephesians 4:25.

It is not enough just to stop lying. To eliminate the negative elements of life and be in a state of neutrality is not sufficient to reach the state of being a new man. It is necessary to incorporate the positive elements into one's life. See Romans 12:21. It is not enough to remain quiet. An indispensable part of honesty is speaking the truth. This is also obligatory when discussing the truth with others. The new man will not be on the side of error, nor will he be satisfied to take a neutral position. He clearly defines his position and makes it evident that he is on the side of truth.

We have been dealing with the matter of speaking and communicating the truth, but truth also has to do with relationships. Besides the objective elements of revelation, which always are truthful, when truth is communicated, it also bears with it the element of a good relationship.

An honest, truthful relationship will exist among believers. As the Christian has Christ in his life and lives with Him, he will not express himself in a way that is not truthful. Lying is incompatible with Christian character and the union that the Christian experiences with Christ. The telling of falsehoods would separate him from Christ as well as from his brethren, and this he does not want.

Lying destroys one's relationship to truth, even though the other party, the object of the lie, may not know about it. The reason for this is that lying makes an internal wound in the person who has told the lie. He knows that he has lied. It has destroyed his inner dignity, and without this he cannot maintain honest relationships.

Paul says that we must speak the truth because "we are members one of another." Ephesians 4:25. The apostle had stated before that we are members of the body of Christ; now he describes unity in personal terms. Each believer bears a relationship to his fellow believer. The telling of falsehoods destroys this relationship.

No matter what kind of lie it is, whether it be lying in a business deal, telling a falsehood to an associate, or distorting the truth in the field of theology, all these are destructive and tear down unity. The new man does not do these kinds of things. He stands firmly on the side of truth and communicates the truth so that complete unity can be achieved among his fellow members in the church.

Not Sinning

The next element in the life of the new man that Paul calls to our attention has been rather perplexing to some readers of the Epistle to the Ephesians. He says, "Be ye angry, and sin not: let not the sun go down upon your wrath: neither give place to the devil." Ephesians 4:26, 27.

The main idea in this phrase is the counsel to "sin not." Many put the emphasis on the phrase "be angry," and then ask, "You mean that the apostle allows us to be short-tempered?" The answer is No. Several verses farther down Paul says, "Let all bitterness, and wrath, and anger . . . be put away from you." Ephesians 4:31. If the new man should not be angry, this cannot be one of his traits of character.

"But," someone says, "Paul says, 'Be ye angry.' " There must be some sort of anger we are allowed to express. What is the difference between this kind of anger and the anger he warns against farther on in the chapter?

The difference is that the first one is not sinful anger. It evidently is similar to the anger God is said to have against unrighteousness. It is that anger that manifests itself in zeal for God in the face of open disregard of righteousness. Moses manifested this kind of anger when the Israelites worshiped the golden calf. Christ manifested similar anger toward those who were profaning His Father's house. See Exodus 32:19; John 2:13-16. This is not the anger of vengeance. "Dearly beloved, avenge not yourselves, but rather give place unto wrath: for it is written, Vengeance is mine; I will repay, saith the Lord." Romans 12:19.

Vengeance belongs to God, and man should not take this divine prerogative upon himself.

Paul is here alluding to Psalm 4:4, where it says, "Stand in awe, and sin not." The new man is concerned for his neighbor. He may be provoked by his neighbor's actions, but he reacts against the sin, not the sinner. But even this "provocation" does not last long: "Let not the sun go down upon your wrath [literally, "provocation," from *parorgismo*]." Ephesians 4:26. The important thing is that the Christian must not sin even when he is offended or provoked.

The sin that Paul mentions here could be compared to shooting arrows at a target and missing the mark. A Christian's actions must not be wasted. When they are, he becomes enervated, and this hinders the development of Christian character. His activities endeavor to hit the target, to reach the mark. Actions that are constructive, that reach their objective, are the kind that are accomplished when Christ is in one's mind. Anything else is the product of an empty mind, aimless, ever missing the target of the upright life.

Vengeful exhibitions of anger fit into this category. Vengeful actions may be energetic, and, for the moment, they may seem to be an effective means of reaching the mark, but it is violent and destructive, and partakes of the old man. From the personal point of view, wreaking vengeance can do nothing to build character. To the contrary, it destroys. Looking at it from the angle of the community, acts of vengeance separate people and destroy unity. The new man does not waste his energy in this kind of activity. His life is full of action, but these actions are constructive, not destructive.

Working and Giving

The preoccupation that Paul has concerning church unity is made evident again in the following principle he lists concerning the conduct of the new man: "Let him that stole steal no more: but rather let him labour, working with his hands the thing which is good, that he may have to give to him that needeth." Ephesians 4:28.

Stealing affects the relationship one has with his neighbor. This act is engraved on the conscience of the one who steals. Every time he sees the person he has robbed, his attitudes are affected by that which has been registered on his mind. He tends to avoid that person's company. He prefers to keep his distance from him physically because he is spiritually distant from him.

The true Christian does not steal. He makes an honest living. As he works, he depends upon God to bless him, and so he is productive. God is present imparting strength and blessing. The man is productive, and his earnings are multiplied beyond his personal needs.

The Christian does not find satisfaction in laboring for personal gain alone. He finds gratification in using the fruit of his labor to help others. "Him that needeth" can be any human being, but primarily it is he with whom "we are members one of another." Ephesians 4:25. Let us remember that Paul is not speaking in terms of solving the poverty problem of the whole world. Neither is he giving a lesson in beneficence on behalf of the needy who exist throughout the world. He is speaking about unity in the church and what its members should do to make this unity effective and enduring.

Speaking Constructively

Constructive words are good words. They are not corrupted. "Let no corrupt communication proceed out of your mouth, but that which is good to the use of edifying, that it may minister grace unto the hearers." Ephesians 4:29.

Corrupt words are spoken by corrupt people because "unto them that are defiled and unbelieving is nothing pure; but even their mind and conscience is defiled. They profess that they know God; but in works they deny him, being abominable, and disobedient, and unto every good work reprobate." Titus 1:15, 16. Those who practice this are unbelievers, godless, abominable, rebellious, and enemies of good works.

Such persons are prone to participate in verbal disputes, but they do not speak the "wholesome words . . . of our Lord Jesus Christ" nor do their words conform to the "doctrine which is according to godliness." Their understanding is corrupt, and their words lack truthfulness. They may not like to appear ungodly. They may even be looked upon as pious because they think that by doing so they will receive material benefits. See 1 Timothy 6:3.

Anything that deviates from the plain word of the Lord is corrupt. The true Christian avoids expressing opinions about truth that has not been clearly revealed, for he does not want to provoke arguments. Arguments cause division in the church, and divisions tear down. The Christian is careful always to speak words that build up—words that are constructive. The true believer speaks only good words—words that contribute toward edification. Thus, the words we speak to our neighbors should be kind and courteous. Our words should never be impetuous, mean, or offensive, and certainly they should never be misleading or untrue. If we are truly living as new creatures, as people worthy of our vocation, we will only speak words that are in harmony with such a life.

Some professed Christians say things to their neighbors that make them think negatively about themselves and others. Such words are upsetting and destroy relationships with others. Do we use words in jest, to make fun of others? Often words that are said jokingly or in fun can be cruel. The people to whom they are directed often do not take them as a joke.

Sometimes words are spoken at social gatherings that ridicule someone. This does not build good relations with others. It only destroys. On the other hand, when one speaks intelligent, thoughtful words, everyone within hearing of them is made happy. Words that express ridicule, words that are cruel, angry, sarcastic, are words that hurt and destroy. They grieve the Holy Spirit. The Holy Spirit is the One who seals us, and we do not want to offend Him.

The Holy Spirit will help the true Christian to know just what words are appropriate to speak to his neighbor and will help him know how to talk to God. In our prayers He helps us to use just the right words. The Holy Spirit clears our minds so that we know just how to express ourselves.

When the tongue uses corrupt words it is a "fire, a world of iniquity: so is the tongue among our members, that it defileth the whole body, and setteth on fire the course of nature; and it is set on fire of hell. . . . The tongue can no man tame; it is an unruly evil, full of deadly poison." James 3:6-8.

The true Christian, he who has been born again, is wise and judicious in what he says. His is not a formal or empty wisdom.

He is prudent and careful in his use of words because he has a transformed heart and a mind that is filled with Christ.

Forgiving as God Forgives

There are certain elements that precede the act of forgiveness: (1) there is a vital relationship with the Holy Spirit; (2) all bitterness, wrath, anger, clamoring, evil speaking, and malice have been cast out of the life; (3) one is kind and tenderhearted to others. See Ephesians 4:30-32. There is also a guiding principle in meting out forgiveness to others: "Forgiving one another, even as God for Christ's sake hath forgiven you." Ephesians 4:32; see also Matthew 6:12.

The culminating feature of the behavior of the new man, the born-again Christian, the one who is reconciled to God, the one who lives worthy of the vocation to which he is called, is his capacity to forgive. When he experiences the new creation "in righteousness and true holiness" (Ephesians 4:24), that is, when he has been justified by Christ and is being sanctified in the truth, certain principles are evident in his life which show he has been transformed into an integrated member of the Christian community. He does not lie; rather, he maintains a relationship of honesty with the other members of the church. He does not yield to the sin of anger, for this destroys his personal relationship with others. He does not steal, because this alienates him spiritually and physically from the rest of his brethren. Instead, he works in such a productive way that he has sufficient resources to be able to help others who are in need. He does not separate himself from others by speaking negative, offensive, or destructive words to his fellowman. He only speaks good words, words that build up and edify. Besides all this, he exercises a forgiving spirit, and this truly identifies him with the community. Forgiving the faults of others is the most positive and congenial way to create unity.

All these qualities are indispensable for the maintenance of unity in the church. However, the capacity to pardon seems to be the most effective means of all. Pardon must be given freely, just as God gives it. See Matthew 18:35. When Christ taught us to ask God's forgiveness in the Lord's Prayer, He said that we should ask for that same measure of forgiveness which we extend to others—"Forgive us our debts, *as we forgive our* debtors." Matthew 6:12, emphasis supplied. Now that the apostle is teaching believers to forgive, he turns it around in order to show how we should pardon others, by saying we must forgive "one another, *even as God for Christ's sake hath forgiven you.*" Ephesians 4:32, emphasis supplied. We are to pardon to the same extent that we are pardoned.

If we do not forgive, we cannot be forgiven. If we forgive much, we will receive abundant forgiveness in return. It is logical, then, that the apostle urges us to extend unlimited pardon to others just as God does, for, if we do, we will also be abundantly pardoned. The Christian should never act like the unjust servant who owed the king a vast sum of money. The servant was forgiven abundantly, but he refused to forgive a fellow servant who owed him only a small debt. Because of his unforgiving spirit, he lost the pardon that he had gained and was alienated from his friends, his fellow servants, his debtor, and from the king, his creditor. He was completely separated from the community when he was sent to prison. See Matthew 18:23-35.

Paul, in speaking of forgiveness, shows us how to become an integral part of the church and how to avoid being separated from it. True pardon is freely given. It is not just a polite, formal act, for he points out that real forgiveness comes from one who is kind and tenderhearted. This is the only way one can be closely knit with the church and contribute to the unity of the believers.

The new man lives and communicates truth, he does not practice sin, he does not steal, he works and shares what he earns with those who are in need, he speaks only that which edifies, and he freely forgives others just as God freely forgives him.

How to Shun Moral Corruption

 # 10(5)

3-8-86

In his Epistle to the Ephesians, Paul gives us advice and counsel on many varied subjects. In the great themes of the epistle—the church, Christ, unity—he describes the principles of living the Christian life. He also refers to the moral life of the believers. See Ephesians 5:1-20.

Imitators of God

The apostle begins this theme by laying the following foundation: "Be imitators of God, as beloved children." Ephesians 5:1, RSV. Imitators? Is it possible to imitate God?

In this sentence the apostle specifies the basic reason for living a clean, moral life: We are the sons and daughters of God and He loves us. Because of this fact, we should imitate Him. Our children imitate us only when they are small, when they are still innocent and free from all hatred and resentment.

Every year our youth department in Brazil presents a special program for both Mother's Day and Father's Day. One year it featured a 30-second TV "spot" which showed a small boy imitating his father. Daddy was in the bathroom shaving, and his son, peeking around the corner, was doing the same thing. A little later Daddy went to the living room and put some things in their proper place. His little son, following behind him, was doing the same thing. Then his father went out to work in the garden. His footprints could be seen in the freshly tilled soil. His son put on an

old pair of Daddy's shoes and was shown walking behind his father, carefully stepping in his footprints.

This demonstration, of course, was a hint to parents to live in
such a way that, as their children imitated them, they too would
live a good life. Children are great imitators of their parents. Especially is this true before they reach the age when they acquire
feelings of hatred and resentment. This is the way the Christian is
to imitate God. This is the way we should duplicate the life that
has no malice.

Living in Love

We must imitate God as children of God, without malice. As
we imitate God we are forming the basis for moral living. The
apostle then says, "Walk in love, as Christ also hath loved us,
and hath given himself for us an offering and a sacrifice to God
for a sweetsmelling savour." Ephesians 5:2.

Love is essential to life. Tests have demonstrated that small
infants can actually die for lack of love. Love is essential for
adults as well, although they do not usually die physically for the
lack of it.

Do you remember when you fell in love for the first time? Everything was the same and yet everything seemed changed. When
we fall in love with a person, that person becomes special to us.
Before we fell in love, the loved one was just another person, but
when love was born, through some mysterious chemistry that de-
fies explanation, we began to see that person in a different light.
He or she looked the same, walked the same, talked the same,
acted the same, yet that person was not the same. Love made the
difference.

What a tragedy that many people, in the name of love, destroy
all possibility of living love deeply and happily. In their great
desire to express their love, they forget that there is a proper time
and place for everything. There is nothing wrong with the expression of physical love, if it is expressed within the marriage relationship, in tender affection for the loved one, and under the right
circumstances. But love falls to pieces when these three aspects
are not taken into consideration. But there is another critical fac-

tor, which in some respects is more important than these. This is the religious aspect. This factor is so important because it has to do with the clear expression of God's will regarding the matter.

Avoiding Immoral Acts and Words

In the area of sex there are sins of actions as well as sins of words. The apostle commands, "But fornication, and all uncleanness, or covetousness, let it not be once named among you, as becometh saints; neither filthiness, nor foolish talking, nor jesting, which are not convenient: but rather giving of thanks." Ephesians 5:3,4. Pure, proper communication is deep and meaningful. Love that is communicated verbally is a love that is transmitted by the personality. The one who communicates only physically is limited.

God's intent is that physical communication of love be postponed until the proper time—a time of full and lifelong commitment of two people to each other. A time when, if children are welcomed into the family, the parents will be prepared to assume parental responsibilities. These would include the conception of the child, his birth, his education for living in this present world and also training him for eternal life.

When Paul refers to immoral words, he makes special mention of "foul talk and coarse jokes." Ephesians 5:4, LB. These are things that are repeated so freely in today's society that they have become commonplace and accepted by many. This type of conversation adversely affects the thinking that leads to immoral practices.

Pornography, although known in Paul's day as depicted on the walls of Pompeii, was not as widespread and rampant as today. Today the media constantly bombard the public with various forms of sex. The tragedy is that some professed Christians indulge their fantasies watching such exhibitions and excuse themselves because they witness these scenes in the privacy of their bedrooms. Is it any wonder that, because "iniquity . . . abound[s], the love of many . . . wax[es] cold" (Matthew 24:12) and we have so many divorces? But this is not all. Love, not only physical love, but love for God and His church waxes cold. By beholding we do become changed (see 2 Corinthians 3:18). What, one might ask, is the difference between lusting after a woman (or a man, for that matter) in the privacy of one's bedroom and lusting after a woman (or a man) out on the street?

Avoiding Those Who Deceive

Not only should we avoid immoral acts and words, but we must also avoid those who practice deception. "Let no man deceive you with vain words: for because of these things cometh the wrath of God upon the children of disobedience. Be not ye therefore partakers with them. For ye were sometimes darkness, but now are ye light in the Lord: walk as children of light: (for the fruit of the Spirit is in all goodness and righteousness and truth;) proving what is acceptable unto the Lord." Ephesians 5:6-10.

Paul is here referring to moral deceivers—those who deceive by their words and teachings, those who teach things that do not express divine wisdom. In some societies and even some churches young people are taught that there is nothing wrong with having premarital sex. The claim is made that sexual continence is detrimental to mental and physical health. These theories are propagated everywhere, including centers of higher learning. But such teachings are contrary to the revealed Word of God. They are false and deceptive.

The lives of those who have practiced illicit sex reveals that they usually have the same health problems as those who do not, if not more. The fact that those who lived in past generations, when such practices were not indulged, yet suffered no physical or mental damage proves the falsity of this theory.

The apostle Paul also declares that he who commits fornication, sins against his own body. See 1 Corinthians 6:18. God and the apostle knew very well that life in close and full relationship with Him, a life in which love for God is enduring, is the only life that is truly happy.

Paul warns: "Have no fellowship with the unfruitful works of darkness, but rather reprove them. For it is a shame even to speak of those things which are done of them in secret. But all things that are reproved are made manifest by the light: for whatsoever doth make manifest is light. Wherefore he saith, Awake thou that sleepest, and arise from the dead, and Christ shall give thee light." Ephesians 5:11-14.

Walking With the Wise

The apostle concludes his instruction on how to avoid immorality by saying, "See then that ye walk circumspectly, not as fools, but as wise, redeeming the time, because the days are evil. Wherefore be ye not unwise, but understanding what the will of the Lord is." Ephesians 5:15-17.

Wisdom is not a common virtue. Nevertheless, a foolish act is easily recognized for what it is. There are some foolish acts that everyone in his right mind avoids at whatever the cost. However, other acts that may not have immediate consequences, but may be just as dangerous in the long run, trap the unwary.

Some years ago I was asked to be guest speaker at a certain school. Before I went onto the platform, a group of girls presented me with a rather large bouquet of flowers. It was their way of showing respect and affection. I went onto the platform holding the flowers in my arms. As I stood there, the flowers and I were the focus of attention. I cannot say I especially enjoyed the rather awkward situation, but, what would have happened if I had thrown the flowers down on the floor and carelessly walked on them? It certainly would have disappointed the young women and shocked the audience. To have done so would have shown extreme insensitivity. I would have shown myself to be a very indifferent, unfeeling, ungrateful person.

Flowers, of course, don't feel; people do. Furthermore, they are worth much more than flowers. When we destroy people, we really destroy ourselves, whether or not we realize it. When we trample on others, we reveal insensitivity worse than that of destroying a bouquet of flowers. But there is another way we can destroy love. We can destroy it by interpretations and customs that are foreign to Christianity.

Among Christians the expression of love should be joyous and happy. A Christian will never cause needless suffering by his words or acts, yet some professedly Christian wives have been known to show vindictiveness by denying their husbands sexual privileges. This is a serious mistake. The excuses some use may seem very reasonable—"If I am not spiritually united with my husband, I cannot have a true sexual relationship with him." But this is not a valid reason for denying one's spouse conjugal rights. The apostle Paul counsels that in such instances a wife should not separate from her husband. (See 1 Corinthians 7:11-16.) The clear implication is that sexual relations were to continue.

The apostle's counsel relative to sexual matters is not only for wives, he also has words of admonition for husbands. They are not only to love their spouses (see Ephesians 3:33), they are also to harbor no bitterness against them (see Colossians 3:19). Sexual relations between spouses should be spontaneous and affectionate—the product of love. The Christian husband tells his wife that she is the dearest woman in the world—and means it—and he shows that he means it by the courteous way he treats her.

Here are some questions a Christian husband should ask himself: To whom does he speak his most gracious words, free from all rudeness? Is it to his wife? Or does she hear only crude words said in private or perhaps in the presence of his children?

The moral life builds happiness. Christian couples should be the happiest in the world. This makes sense—the love of God is shed abroad in their hearts. See Romans 5:5.

Women, as a rule, have a much deeper capacity for love than men have. Poets extol their tenderness. They should use these talents on their husbands. A wife should make her husband feel that she is totally and solely in love with him.

The moral life consists of more than avoiding immorality. It is the proper expression of complete love. Love will motivate us to dispel the dark shadows in the corners of our lives. It will kindle the joys of life and liven the monotony of daily routine. True love creates unity in the family. To achieve it, we need to be "filled with the Spirit." Ephesians 5:18.

Let us pray to God that we may live a love replete with spirituality, a love impregnated with true communication, a love that imparts to life all its joy, all its fullness, a love that in all its beauty and freedom is like the love in the heart of God which is truly beautiful and free.

How to Safeguard Family Unity

(J: 22 -
   33)

#11
3-15-86

In this chapter we will study Ephesians 5:21 through 6:9. Here the apostle Paul addresses each member of the family, telling him what he should do to preserve family unity. After the individual, the family is the basic unit of the church and society. Complete unity in the church is possible only if there is also unity in the family.

The apostle's counsel embraces, not only the Ephesian Christians, but all who constitute a part of a family in our day—the father, the mother, the children, and even the servants, where there are such. Before the apostle addresses each member of the family, he sets forth a general principle applicable to all: "Submit to one another out of reverence for Christ." Ephesians 5:21 NIV. Here the apostle teaches that in the sight of God all members of the family stand on an equal footing, and this is shown by each family member showing deference to every other family member. This rules out all arbitrary despotism or authoritarianism exercised by one member of the family over the others. All render voluntary submission to the others for the common good, in the fear of the Lord.

The Wife: Submissive but Not Inferior

Paul says, "Wives, submit to your husbands as to the Lord. For the husband is the head of the wife as Christ is the head of the church, his body, of which he is the Saviour. Now as the church submits to Christ, so also wives should submit to their husbands in everything." Ephesians 5:22-24, NIV.

Submit is the key word that describes the relationship of the wife to her husband. This word has been a big problem to many people and, without a doubt, it lies at the root of many of the injustices that have been shown toward women. To really understand this term we must first take note that Paul does not direct these words to the men. He does not say, "Husbands, submit yourselves to your wives." The apostle is talking to the wives. This verse, however, gives the husband no authority to treat his wife as a slave that must do everything he demands of her.

The word *submit* is on a par with the word *love* used by Paul when he directs his remarks to the husbands. See Ephesians 5:25. Both indicate a voluntary giving of themselves one to the other.

The attitude of the wife submitting voluntarily to her husband complements the attitude of the husband who loves his wife. Each spouse plays a distinctive role in the relationship. The wife recognizes the husband as the head of the family, and he in turn loves his wife with the same kind of love that Christ has for His church. In the reciprocity of the love relationship no problem arises in Paul's statement that "the husband is the head of the wife." Ephesians 5:23, NIV.

How is the husband the head of the wife? In the same verse it tells us, "as Christ is the head of the church." If there is still a question in one's mind about this, if one still doesn't understand, the apostle Paul explains it further by saying, "The husband is the head of the wife as Christ is the head of the church, his body, of which he is the Savior." Verse 23.

Just as Christ is head of the church in order to save it, the husband must be head of his wife in order to protect and save her. Salvation is the basis of the relationship of Christ to the church. Everything that Christ does, He does for the good of His church. He does not give a single command to the church simply for the purpose of showing that He is superior to it. If He gives a command, He does so for the best interests of the church. The relationship of Saviour-saved is not the relationship of chief-subordinate. Everything that comes from the head in this relationship is for the good of the body. This is equally true of the husband-wife relationship. A husband's every thought and act relative to his wife is for her good and happiness.

In the sight of God both spouses are equal: "There is neither male nor female: for ye are all one in Christ Jesus." Galatians 3:28. Yet, in harmony with the divine plan (see Genesis 3:16), the wife voluntarily submits to her husband. She has chosen to live with the man who is her husband, and she accepts him as head of their family. Even before sin entered the world, God created a wife for Adam, saying, "It is not good that the man should be alone; I will make him an help meet for him." Genesis 2:18; see 1 Corinthians 11:9.

What is a "help meet"? It does not mean a helper in the sense that Eve and her daughters were to be treated as inferior beings, receiving orders from their husbands. A help meet is a person completely capable of helping someone else. The expression does not place the wife on a lower level than her husband. Some men who read the apostle's words place the emphasis on the word *help* and forget the word *meet*. The Hebrew word, *neged,* literally translates, "as in front of him," meaning "his counterpart." In other words, Eve was made to complement Adam.

In the Old Testament God is described as man's "helper." See Psalm 33:20; 46:1; 121:1, 2. Does this mean that God is inferior to man? No. It means that he complements man, supplying his needs for accomplishing the divine purpose. In a similar way, the wife complements her husband in fulfilling his role as head of the family. In no way is she inferior to her husband. Nor is she superior to him. She is fully her husband's equal, although in the divine plan he is first among equals.

The Husband: Loves Like Christ Loves

Paul addresses the husbands by saying, "Husbands, love your wives." Ephesians 5:25, RSV. This is the same kind of intimate relationship, the giving of oneself, that Paul referred to when he spoke to the wives. The question now is, How could Paul be speaking about the husband's giving of himself to his wife, if he is not speaking of love? The Christian husband gives of himself to the utmost. The verse goes on to say that the husband should "love . . . *as Christ loved* the church and gave himself up for her." Ephesians 5:25, RSV. Christ gave His all to save the church, and He is her protector. Even so husbands should give their all for their wives and should be their protectors. It is in this sense that the husband is the "savior" of the wife. Love is the motivating force in everything that the Christian husband does for his wife.

When a man marries, he enters into a new relationship in which he gets to really truly know the woman he has chosen to be his wife. He will probably discover that she has some faults and shortcomings that he had not been aware of—defects of character that he had not observed before. What should he do? Reject his wife? No. Like every other human being he has his faults too. So, with love he overlooks her faults, he protects her from the criticisms of others, and he helps her overcome her weaknesses. At the same time, she overlooks his faults, protects his reputation, and helps him to be an overcomer.

In a sense the husband assumes the faults of his wife as if they were his own. He has taken her as his own, and now, when he sees her shortcomings ever so clearly, he still accepts her as his wife. This is not just a simple formal acceptance to fulfill the social aspect of marriage; it is accepting the wife with complete love, thus fulfilling the spiritual aspects of marriage. Never should a husband or wife think, much less say, "When I married my spouse, I made a big mistake." Each has vowed to accept the other as a complete person, including the faults.

Mutual criticism and faultfinding only cause division in a marriage. The apostle is anxious that Christian couples maintain their unity and devotion one to the other. This unity involves the personal giving of one's self to the other, the wife voluntarily submitting to her husband and the husband loving his wife with all his heart. And this, even to the point of sacrifice, if need be—even unto death.

The Children: Obedient to Maintain Family Unity

Paul's admonition to the children might seem out of date in this permissive age, but it still holds true for Christian households. "Children, obey your parents in the Lord: for this is right. Honour thy father and mother; which is the first commandment with promise; that it may be well with thee, and thou mayest live long on the earth." Ephesians 6:1-3.

Many children today hardly know the word *obedience*. However, the Christian son or daughter understands this admonition. He does not hold the same philosophy as his non-Christian peers. He knows that long ago the apostle predicted that "in the last days perilous times [would] come. For men . . . [would] be . . . disobedient to parents." 2 Timothy 3:1, 2. We live in a time of disobedience. Many children refuse to obey their parents.

In this passage the apostle Paul is obviously speaking of unregenerate children. This prophecy provides all the more reason for Christian children to be obedient. "Children, obey your parents *in the Lord:* for this is right." Ephesians 6:1, emphasis supplied. Observe that this injunction implies that there may be circumstances under which children are not required to obey their parents. These circumstances only arise when parents require obedience in a matter that is clearly contrary to the Lord's revealed will. For example, Paul's admonition does not require a Christian son or daughter to violate the eighth commandment, "Thou shalt not steal." Exodus 20:15. Obedience to parents is to be "in the Lord."

Fathers: Discipline Without Provoking

Parents must learn how to discipline their children without discouraging them. They must learn that continual scolding and nagging is counterproductive. Positive example generally produces better results. Negative talk tends to arouse anger and resentment. Paul's solution is for Christian parents to rear their children "with the loving discipline the Lord himself approves, with suggestions and godly advice." Ephesians 6:4, LB.

Many parents are prone to be impatient with their children's religious progress. After all what Christian parent would not like to see his children be Christians from their very birth! But this does not happen very often. See Luke 1:15. What parents can do is provide the best possible spiritual environment for their children. Even then this is no guarantee that a child will make the right choice. However, a truly Christian home environment greatly increases the chances that the right choice will be made.

The home should be a genuine Christian community. If the father and mother act as true shepherds of the flock, they will exercise such a positive influence over their children that they will be closely united in the home and live in perfect unity with the church. This calls for true conversion on the part of the parents. The Spirit of God can create in parents the proper attitudes and through His work the parents can be enabled to exercise discipline without provocation.

Servant and Masters: Render Obedience and Exercise Authority With Love

The last relationship that the apostle Paul describes in this section of his epistle, is the relationship that the parents, as masters, should maintain toward servants in the family. In Paul's day servants were slaves *(doulos)* and were considered part of the family. In our day we do not have slaves, although in some households and in some cultures servants do the domestic chores. In such situations servants do not usually become part of the family. Nevertheless, the principles expounded by the apostle can be applied in some aspects of our present day society. Whether we are employees or employers, we have certain obligations to one another, although not that of master and slave.

Thus, Paul counsels employees to obey their earthly employers and "be eager to give them [their] very best" (Ephesians 6:5, LB), doing their tasks with the same faithful dedication they would show in serving Christ. Efficiency in one's work has always been a highly prized virtue in the Christian world. Work done from the heart not only pleases the employer, but it also produces a certain sense of satisfaction in the employee.

On the other hand, the employer must not use threats or force. The reason for this admonition is that all are equal in God's sight. Whether employer or employee, all are servants of the Lord, and He shows no partiality or favoritism. If Christians will adopt this principle, they will be surprised at the spirit of unity and cooperation it will engender. As a result employers and employees will be more productive in their work. There are benefits for everyone. Relationships with one another will be more pleasant, more compatible, and more Christian.

To sum up: Family unity is achieved and maintained when the husband and his wife give themselves completely to each other, when the wife submits herself voluntarily to her husband and her husband loves her with the same devotion as Christ loves His church. The children obey their parents because this is right and because by so doing they are helping to preserve family unity. Parents should discipline their children in love, lest they discourage them. They correct them with tenderness and affection. Employers and employees should remember that both are servants of Christ and that by exercising Christian principles they will please God and will experience greater unity.

How to Live a
Victorious Life

#/2
3-22-86
Eph 6: 1-9

Every Christian needs to live a victorious life. No one, however, enjoys such perfect spiritual health that he can dispense with
the divine power that enables him to do better. There are times
when Christians experience defeat. There are times, when like
Peter walking on the water, they take their eyes off the Saviour.
At such times they stumble before the onslaughts of the enemy.
As a result they are overcome with feelings of distress and remorse. And yet, in the midst of his agony and self-condemnation,
the true Christian says to himself, "By God's grace, I won't ever
do that again."

And then he starts the battle all over again with all his might
and main.

Strength for the Victory

Resolve and determination alone are not the solution to overcoming sin. The apostle says, "Finally, my brethren, be strong *in
the Lord,* and *in the power of his might.*" Ephesians 6:10, emphasis supplied. We have to "be strong in the Lord" if we are to
experience victory in the Christian life. It is extremely necessary
to be determined in our own minds. We ought to be. But this
alone is not sufficient for achieving victory in the Christian life.
Determination, however, is useful in putting us on the right track.

Our victory has to be gained through power that comes from
the Lord. When the Christian does not place his life, his will, in
connection with enabling power, he is bound to fall sooner or

later. A victorious life is possible for everyone who keeps His eyes on Jesus. Only He, not determination, not willpower, can keep us from falling. See Jude 24. Infinite power to overcome is always there, but sometimes we fail to avail ourselves of it. And when we do, we fall a prey to Satan's temptations.

The Christian's warfare is spiritual. See Ephesians 6:12. The enemy is always near at hand to tempt. He aims his "fiery arrows" at us (Ephesians 6:16, LB), intending to destroy us, and our only safety is in putting on "the whole armour of God." Ephesians 6:13.

Paul shows us the way to win the fight of faith. After his personal decision to serve God with all his heart and soul, the Christian must put on all the armor of God. Only thus is victory sure.

Withstanding in the Evil Day

Paul counsels: Take all God's armor that you might withstand in "the evil day." Ephesians 6:13. What is this evil day? It is a dark day. It is any day. It is every moment, every circumstance in this present life. While life lasts this battle never ceases—never reaches a truce.

Whenever the Christian thinks that everything is going just fine and he can take it easy a little while, it is then that the enemy surprises him and defeats him. David was a seasoned veteran in fighting "the battles of the Lord." He always came out conqueror when he fought in the name of the Lord and was accompanied by the Lord of hosts. David usually trusted in God's power. There was no bear or lion or Philistine, no giant or "nongiant" that could resist the strength of the young soldier who fought the battles of the Lord with the power that came from Him. But, there on the palace roof, when David was spending some leisure time, while his soldiers were off to war, the devil inscribed the darkest pages, the most disastrous defeat, in David's life. That chapter entailed grave consequences. It cost David considerable pain to turn over that page and become a victor once more. It cost him suffering, remorse, and recrimination. And, he suffered the effects in his own home when he saw his sons openly commit sins that he had committed in secret.

When the Christian sits down to rest, he is laying the stage for a defeat. The evil day Paul talks about can be any time, any moment. The Christian must be on his guard at all times.

The Armor of Victory

After having spoken about the need to be on guard against the "evil day," Paul tells the Christian about the armor he must put on. There are six pieces of armor, and they are described in two groups of three.

In the first group are truth, righteousness, and the gospel. See Ephesians 6:14, 15. Righteousness is listed between the truth and the gospel. This seems to say that when the Christian receives the truth and accepts the gospel, along with them he receives righteousness. Certainly this is so. Truth and the gospel are synonymous.

Truth is a revelation from God. The gospel is the good news that brings the message of redeeming truth. Both the truth and the gospel are related to the person of Christ. They speak about a Saviour—about His suffering, His love, His victory. They give assurance to those who are in Christ Jesus, that they also shall obtain the victory. He who accepts the truth and the gospel also receives righteousness from the Lord. "Being justified by faith, we have peace with God through our Lord Jesus Christ." Romans 5:1.

Then comes the second group. Faith, salvation, and the Word of God. See Ephesians 6:16, 17. If the other pieces of armor were important, these are absolutely essential. Paul says, "Above all." If it was invaluable to have truth, righteousness, and the gospel, it is absolutely essential to have faith, salvation, and the Word.

The apostle undergirds all these pieces of armor with prayer: "Praying always with all prayer and supplication in the Spirit." Ephesians 6:18. The Christian must live and move in the atmosphere of prayer if he is to be victorious. Unfortunately, we do not always ground all our personal and corporate activities on prayer. Too many times we base them on a deceiving kind of self-confidence but such self-confidence can lead to our spiritual undoing.

Satan's most successful attacks against the church usually come from within its ranks. Often these attacks originate among those who are well trained in theology and in the doctrines of the church. The attacks of these agents on the fundamental tenets of the church are usually camouflaged under a show of great piety and in the name of "intellectual honesty." They profess not to be able to hold the church's fundamental beliefs and at the same time be intellectually honest.

One would think that, if this were truly the case, these agents would voluntarily withdraw from a body, with the fundamental teachings of which they are in disagreement, but usually they do not. In many cases they are paid employees of the church who continue to receive their salary from the church, while at the same time attacking the church, and all, of course, in the name of "intellectual honesty."

In apostolic times there were rebels who liked to "have the preeminence among them." 3 John 9. But the apostolic leaders rejected these rebels and rebuked them. Their forthright counsel to the faithful ones was, "If there come any unto you, and bring not this doctrine, receive him not into your house, neither bid him God speed: for he that biddeth him God speed is partaker of his evil deeds." 2 John 10, 11.

In these days of earth's history many are all too aware of the form of godliness but are ignorant of practical religion. Many search the Scriptures merely to find arguments to sustain their doctrinal differences. They do not read the Bible in order to get in touch with God—the One who revealed, who communicated this Word. They read its pages only to be sharper in their debates, more powerful in the presentation of their ideas, more incisive in the pet ideas they are defending.

Then there are those who read their Bibles just in order to point out what is wrong with the church. They criticize the leaders, the structure, the procedures, the decision-making process. Everything about the church is criticized. Whoever does not criticize is thought to be old-fashioned or ignorant or incompetent. They are considered "unfaithful" to the church or mentally deficient. But the Bible was not revealed to us for this purpose. It was revealed that we might be in contact with the eternal God who made the heavens and the earth and who gave His Son to save the lost.

There are many aspects to the struggles that confront the Christian today, but he can be victorious. How? By putting on the whole armor of God. He needs every part of this armor. None of it can safely be laid aside or discarded.

A Living Study of the Scriptures

We need to study the Scriptures in an attitude of love and devotion. We need to read the Bible like someone who has just received a love letter and is eagerly reading it. One who does this may be ignorant concerning history, he may not be able to comprehend anything about geography, he may feel inadequate when it comes to mathematics, he may be a "know-nothing" in the field of literature, he may be able to retain little of the information he reads in books, but, when he receives a letter from someone with whom he has fallen in love, it matters not how long it is, he reads it through at once, at one sitting, then reads it again and again until he knows it by heart.

Is it any wonder that afterwards he is able to recount each idea, each expression, every detail of the letter's message? Being in love has a way of indelibly impressing itself on one's memory. When this mysterious process takes place, some people are surprised. "How," they ask, "can a person with such a meager intellectual capacity remember so much?" It is the same person. He has the same intelligence as before. Talk to him about anything else and he may not be able to comprehend it. But talk to him about the contents of that love letter, and he knows it all. What makes the difference? The letter is the focus of his interest. Only one thing matters—the letter from his sweetheart!

We need to read God's love letter to us—the Bible—with the same interest and intensity as a person in love. If we are truly in love with God, His message will be the focus of our attention. We will read it again and again until it becomes a part of us. We will read it with our heart—with a heart that has fallen in love.

Reading the Bible this way, one partakes of its beauty. Such perusal clothes old truth with new meaning. The gospel of Luke could be a starting point. Take your Bible right now and open it to the beginning of Luke's Gospel and read it with a mind open to the divine impressions by the Holy Spirit. What insights such study brings. Let God speak to you through His word and then respond to Him, perhaps as in the following dialog:

"Forasmuch as many have taken in hand to set forth in order a declaration of those things which are most surely believed among us . . . "

Lord, I, too, surely believe these things. I cannot write the story that has already been written, but thank You for writing it for me.

"Even as they delivered them unto us, which from the beginning were eyewitnesses . . . "

Lord, I cannot say that I have seen You with my physical eyes, but I can say that I have seen You with my spiritual eyes. You have been with me so many times, so many times! Thank You for Your abiding presence.

"And ministers of the word . . . "

Yes, You have revealed Yourself to me so many times, and that's exactly the reason why You have made me a minister of Your Word too! I want to faithfully fulfill this ministry. Help me in my weakness. Transform me into an honest, faithful, spiritual, competent minister of Thy Word.

"It seemed good to me also, having had perfect understanding of all things from the very first, to write unto thee in order, most excellent Theophilus . . . "

Lord, help me that I too can present these things in an orderly manner to the many modern Theophiluses who need Your gospel.

We can proceed through the entire Bible this way, carrying on a continual conversation with God. Each morning we can dedicate some time for this kind of reading. Half an hour or more. Whatever amount of time we can spare. It strengthens the spirit. It gives us confidence as we face life's struggles. It keeps the mind alert against temptation. It helps us stand firm in our decisions. The mind is filled with the divine presence, and the Spirit takes control of our thoughts.

When God speaks, He desires a response from His earthly children. He speaks through His Word. He wants to communicate, to converse with us. He doesn't want His Word to be just a monologue which He repeats over and over again, never listening to our response. The main thing we want to get out of our Bible reading is the personal knowledge of its Author. If Bible students used this means of study, there would be less argument about supposed errors. They would act with more reverence before the almighty and magnificent presence of the God of the Sacred Scriptures, and would better understand His will for each one of us.

Victory in Christian warfare is not a victory by argument. It is a victory over sin in the life. Victory is won when we are in league with God. The armor of God is what gives us partnership with Him, His activating power, the presence of His Spirit, and the strength of His might.

Praying at All Times

Besides conversing with God through His Word, we must also talk with Him in prayer. How little we converse with God in prayer! I am not saying that we offer only a few prayers. A typical Adventist participates in about 30 prayers during the week plus 16 prayers in the Sabbath day. I do not say that we pray only a few prayers. I am saying that we converse very little with God.

Paul says, "Praying always with all prayer and supplication in the Spirit." Ephesians 6:18. We must be engaged in prayer all the time. In another place Paul says, "Pray without ceasing." 1 Thessalonians 5:17.

How can we pray without ceasing and at the same time talk with God? A person's mind is in constant activity, except during sleep, and even then it does not entirely stop. It is continually engaged with one thought or another. But by nature, a man's mind soliloquizes—carries on a monologue or one-sided conversation.

In order to carry on a continual conversation with God, all that we need to do is to transform our one-sided monologue of thought into a dialogue with God. We do not need to alter anything. We simply include God in our thinking. The mind is occupied by talking to Him and telling Him everything. It is as if we were carrying on a conversation with someone. This will not reduce the efficiency of our work. Every time our work needs to be coordinated with our thinking, we can tell God exactly what we are doing—tell Him about the work and the thoughts we are thinking about it. The same thing can be done when we are reading a book. When one reads a book, his mind should concentrate on the subject matter, but he can incorporate God into the process. Reading always causes reactions or responses in our thinking. We can tell God about those reactions going on in our mind. Instead of thinking just to ourselves, let us use our minds in dialogue with God.

In this way all of life's circumstances, the common tasks, the routine thinking that goes on in our daily lives, all we do, can be transformed unto a dialogue with God. All of life's aspects—the simple and the complicated, the big and the insignificant—all the things that make up life are transformed into a sanctuary where God is with us and we are talking together. How wonderful life becomes! Common things are transformed into sacred things. It is like Moses' burning bush. A common desert shrub suddenly converted into a sacred, holy encounter. And all because God was there.

As we converse with God, we will go our way with more reverence for life. We will find greater significance in the things that we are doing. We will grow spiritually in everything we do in life. If each member of the church would live in this manner, we would soon have a church full of saints.

Speaking About Christ With Boldness

A life that is in constant touch with God cannot help but speak about Christ. Paul asked the Ephesians to pray for him, "that utterance may be given unto me, that I may open my mouth boldly, to make known the mystery of the gospel, for which I am an ambassador in bonds: that therein I may speak boldly, as I ought to speak." Ephesians 6:19, 20.

To speak boldly is to speak without fear. Without complexes, without restrictions, without inhibitions. We are to speak about Christ just as we would speak concerning personal things. We are to tell others about His life just as we would tell them about our own lives. We are to talk about His great deeds of redemption just as we would talk about the common things happening in our daily lives.

We can tell others about the life of Christ through our personal experience. We can tell what happens to us when He is with us in our work, in our daily struggles, in our temptations, in everything we do.

Wherever we find ourselves, we have a pulpit, whether we are at work, at home, at school. Wherever we are we will be ambassadors of the Lord. Each person with whom we come in contact will have an opportunity to see with his own eyes what happens to a person when he gives himself over completely to God. They cannot help but see what happens when an individual is totally committed to truth, to justice, to the gospel, to faith, to salvation, and to the Word of God. Although he may not continually be on his knees, his life is a life of constant prayer.

The life of the Christian is full of struggles, for his is the object of Satan's attacks. His struggle is not merely "against flesh and blood" (Ephesians 6:12)—human antagonists—but against the "spiritual hosts of wickedness" (RSV). These unseen foes use all their powers to fight against us, but victory is sure for those who resist unto the end. See James 4:7; Matthew 10:22. The days in which we live are days of victory—days of triumph, for it is not in times of peace that armies conquer, but in days of conflict.

Now is the time when we must believe the truth, when we must follow righteousness, when we must proclaim the gospel, when we must experience faith, when we must enjoy salvation, when we must study the Word of God, and when we must live in continual communion with God wherever we find ourselves. Now is the time when our weakness must be made "strong in the Lord, and in the power of His might" (verse 10) so that victory may always be ours.

With Undying Love

#13
7-29-86
Eph 6:10-24

In the closing lines of his epistle, Paul wishes the Ephesians well. Included in his parting words, the apostle makes mention of some things that concern him, and he expresses his heartfelt desires on behalf of a church that he deeply loves. Paul was its founder and its principal pastor. As a result, a bond of affection had developed between the apostle and the Ephesians, and he knew that the church in Ephesus was interested in him.

It is for this reason the apostle says to them: "Tychicus, the dear brother and faithful servant in the Lord, will tell you everything, so that you also may know how I am and what I am doing. I am sending him to you for this very purpose, that you may know how we are, and that he may encourage you.

"Peace to the brothers, and love with faith from God the Father and the Lord Jesus Christ. Grace to all who love our Lord Jesus Christ with an undying love." Ephesians 6:21-24, NIV.

There at its conclusion, the epistle reaches its climax. The apostle summarizes his entire letter in that last phrase, "with an undying love."

Paul is concerned about three things as he writes this conclusion. First of all, he lets the recipients of his letter know that he realizes they are interested in how he is doing, his anxieties, and what he is going through while in prison. In order to let them know, he dispatches a messenger, Tychicus, to tell them how things are coming along, so they will not worry about him. Tychicus will tell them about the work he is doing. He will let them know that he is still carrying on his ministry and is witnessing to others, even though he is in chains. Tychicus will take the news to the church members in Ephesus that they too may be comforted and encouraged.

The apostle's second concern is that the church members in Ephesus will experience peace and love with faith—the peace and love with faith that comes from the Father and the Lord Jesus Christ.

Third, he is concerned about the spiritual life of the Ephesian believers. He wants grace to be with all those who love the Lord Jesus Christ with undying love.

The apostle's last words speak of love. It is therefore fitting that we conclude our study by contemplating this same theme. When Paul says "all who love" (RSV), he is not just speaking to the Ephesian church members, he also includes all believers throughout all time. True Christians love Jesus Christ.

God wants us to love Jesus Christ. He expects His church to love the Lord. But they are not to love Him with just any kind of love. He wants them to love Him with undying love.

A Love That Gives

The love that Paul is describing in the Epistle to the Ephesians is a love that gives. "God is so rich in mercy; he loved us so much that even though we were spiritually dead and doomed by our sins, he gave us back our lives again when he raised Christ from the dead." Ephesians 2:4, 5, LB. It is a love that gives. It gives things. Yes, it is good to give things. But more than giving things, Christian love gives the person of Christ. Together with Christ it gives us life. It raises us up and makes us sit together in heavenly places. Love gives us the experiences of life.

It is not enough to give things. We need to give our own experiences. Love becomes much more evident when we give the experiences of life than when we give things. The things we give manifest love. But how we relate ourselves to others in life has much greater value than the things we can give them.

But there is still something more important that love must give, and this is our very own person. "Walk in love, as Christ also hath loved us, and hath given himself for us." Ephesians 5:2. We must give ourselves in the same way that Christ gave Himself. He gave Himself to serve, to teach, to help, and to save. Love is communicated through the things we give, through the experiences of life that we can offer; but love will never be perfect if we do not give our own person as we communicate. As someone has said, "The gift without the giver is bare."

Each day, each moment, we should offer good opportunities for demonstrating love. At all times we can give things, give experiences in life, give our very own person to others. When others receive Christ through our imparting these gifts of love, they feel our appreciation of them and know that we are interested in them and want the very best for them.

One more activity is necessary for the love that gives. Paul was happy that the church members in Ephesus loved in this manner, for he said, Since "I heard of your faith in the Lord Jesus, and love unto all the saints, [I] cease not to give thanks for you." Ephesians 1:15, 16.

Love must give of itself equally to everyone, without any class distinction or partiality. It is true that in order to be organized and to function with the greatest efficiency, it is necessary to have some sort of structure with different levels of responsibility. For Christians these operational levels exist only for practical purposes. Their only reason for being is to enable the church to be more efficient in its missionary outreach. From God's point of view and from the aspect of Christian love, all the members are equal.

Those who function as leaders in the church, whether in the local church or on other organizational levels, must relate themselves to the others by living out these principles of love. There can be no unity in a church where the leaders act as despots. On the other hand, the other dimension of love must not be overlooked. Church members cannot be cold and indifferent to their leaders. They must love them with the same love that they expect their leaders to show to them.

When one imparts love, he gives everything. The church exists in order to preach the gospel. The gospel is the good news about the love of God, the love of Him who gave His Son for all of us as sinners. This mission must be fulfilled in the spirit of this same kind of love.

Leaders and those under their leadership will undoubtedly commit mistakes, in spite of their best intentions to carry out their mission. These mistakes must be rectified in love. Love does not criticize. It does not misinterpret the actions of others. It does not judge its leaders. It does not condemn those being led.

Love does not show animosity. It does not live in distrust. It does not defame those who are in positions of responsibility who do not especially please us. Love never seeks revenge. It shows good will. It expresses honest satisfaction and appreciation, and it overlooks others' mistakes.

It is right to love all the members of Christ's body all the time, and this especially includes those occasions when they have serious faults. It is easy to love the new members of the church on the day they are baptized. The difficult part is to love them when they deserve discipline for wrong doing. But love makes no distinction in these instances. Even though discipline is necessary, it treats them with kindness and speaks gracious words intended to help strengthen the fallen. While love is never an accomplice in hiding the misdeeds of others, it expresses redemption. While it is concerned with maintaining the purity of the church, it never forgets that the church is a community of repentant sinners who sometimes, unintentionally, fall into sin.

Because of such love, the Christian expresses his feelings in words of encouragement. When those who hear those words ponder them, they always feel better. It strengthens them for the continual struggles they meet day by day.

Each member is in the church in order to live this kind of love. God expects us to be impartial, nondiscriminatory—to manifest the same constant love to everyone.

Love Is the Foundation of the Christian Life

Love that gives things, that gives experiences of life, that gives its own self to others, love that makes no discrimination between persons, is vital to the Christian experience.

Upon that love depends our adoption as God's children (Ephesians 1:4, 5), our sanctification (Ephesians 1:4), our fullness in Christ Jesus (Ephesians 3:19), the spiritual growth of each Christian, individually, and of the church as a community (Ephesians 4:15, 16), as well as the unity of the church. "With all lowliness and meekness, with long-suffering, forbearing one another in love; endeavouring to keep the unity of the Spirit in the bond of peace." Ephesians 4:2, 3.

If so much depends upon love, shouldn't we Christians live it in all its fullness?

Undying Love

The apostle Paul says that we must not only love Christ and our neighbor, but we must love them "with an undying love." The word *undying* is associated with time and with character. That which is undying is constant. It is unchangeable in time and in character.

Someone has said that "love is not love which alters when it alteration finds." True love keeps on loving.

The same word that Paul uses to describe "undying" love is sometimes translated "incorruptible." The apostle He says that Christ brought to light the incorruption of future immortality through the gospel. See 2 Timothy 1:10. He describes the glory of God as "incorruptible." Romans 1:23. He says that the righteous will be resurrected "incorruptible." 1 Corinthians 15:52. Speaking of a woman's adornment, Peter says that it should be "that which is not corruptible, even the ornament of a meek and quiet spirit." 1 Peter 3:4.

Undying love is a love that endures forever. That which is incorruptible is by its very nature eternal. This love maintains the character in complete sanctification because the undying aspect preserves the true relationship with God. The church must have this undying love. It is an imperishable, incorruptible love—a love that is spiritual and eternal.

These words, very appropriately, conclude Paul's epistle. He is asking the faithful ones to become integrated with God, with the church, and with their fellow church members so that there can be complete unity in the body of Christ. The apostle also asks us to live in Christ for the glory of God, and not for our own self-exaltation. All this requires undying love. It requires consecration of time and character. It requires giving the life and the personality.

This complete experiencing of undying love brings unity with Christ and the church, and it endures for ever.